PHILIP MATYSZAK

MEDEA
QUEEN OF WITCHES

Book II in the 'Unauthorised Biography' series

Monashee Mountain Publishing

Philip Matyszak has a doctorate in Roman history from St John's College, Oxford University and is the author of many books on Ancient History including the best-selling *The Greek and Roman Myths: A Guide to the Classical Stories*, *Ancient Athens on Five Drachmas a Day* and *Lost and Forgotten Cities of the Ancient World*. He teaches e-learning courses in Ancient History for the Institute of Continuing Education at Cambridge University. For more information visit: www.matyszakbooks.com

First published in 2024 by Monashee Mountain Publishing (Canada)

Copyright © Philip & Malgosia Matyszak 2024

ISBN 978-0-9881066-9-7

All Rights Reserved. No part of this publication may be copied, reproduced, transferred, distributed in any form or by any means electronic or mechanical except as specifically permitted in writing by the publisher.

The characters in this book are mythical. Any resemblance to anyone not dead for two thousand years is purely coincidental. Unless stated otherwise, all translations of classical works are by the author. The illustrations are adapted from works in the public domain, contributed by private individuals or directly commissioned for this text.

Book Cover by Ravastra Design Studios.
Cover picture based on a Roman fresco of Medea in the Naples National Archaeological Museum.

E-mail: info@ monasheemountainpublishing.com
Website: www.monasheemountainpublishing.com.

This book is dedicated to Barbara Hooley, who is not like Medea, not at all, in any way.

Acknowledgements

Every book is a team project, and I would like to thank those who helped to prepare this book, including those who generously provided photographs and reference material. Particular thanks go to Jeremy Day who provided invaluable comments and edits on the early drafts. Even more thanks are due to my wife Malgosia who not only put up with a husband who went missing in ancient Greece for days on end, but even forgave me enough to edit and lay out the final text.

CONTENTS

Introduction	The Many Faces of Medea	vi
Chapter 1	Searching for Medea: *The Land and People of Colchis*	1
Chapter 2	Arrival of a Flawed Hero: *Jason and the Voyage of the Argo*	20
Chapter 3	Securing the Fleece	39
Chapter 4	The Flight from Colchis	57
Chapter 5	The Long Journey to Greece	75
Chapter 6	The Next Obstacle: *Crete and Talos*	94
Chapter 7	Dark Deeds in Iolcus	112
Chapter 8	A Different World: *Greece in the Heroic Age*	131
Chapter 9	Irreconcilable Differences	151
Chapter 10	Preparations	167
Chapter 11	Murder Most Foul: *And Character Assassination too*	183
Chapter 12	Aftermath	212
Epilogue	Medea's Cultural Afterlife	239
Sources		245
Index		248

Medea the Sorceress by Valentine Cameron Prinsep (1838–1904)

Introduction

The Many Faces of Medea

Murderess, distressed mother, proto-feminist, textbook psychopath – few women in Greek myth have been analysed as closely as the killer queen from Colchis, and few have had their story used so extensively as a platform to propagate the opinions of others.

The story of Medea has been told many times and in many ways. Ancient writers include the Greek playwright Euripides whose treatment was so controversial that, when entered in competition, his seminal work barely scraped into third place - in a field of three. While Euripides tells Medea's story with considerable sympathy, later Romans writers such as Ovid and Seneca the Younger concentrate on the flaws in Medea's character, which were abundant, and the sensational aspects of her life – which was most of it.

Modern writers have also seized upon the story of Medea and the universal themes which it contains – for examples, there's arrogance headed for a fall, passion, scheming and ghastly revenge. Through it all we see that Medea is always apparently destined to be the victim of other people's schemes, yet instead she emerges victorious - partly through her superior skills as a manipulator and partly because she is simply more unreasonably ruthless than anyone could expect. It's great theatre.

There is also something deeply seductive about Medea – she is not just a strong woman, she is a terrifying one who was slightly less safe to be around than an infuriated cobra. The casualty rate among her nearest and dearest resembles that of a front-line combat regiment, yet it remains impossible to see Medea as just a comic-book villain. Generally we can understand her motivation, and part of her appeal is that she does all those things that we stop our darker selves from doing – and she gets away with it.

Ever wanted to kill your annoying younger brother? Medea wanted to, so she did. Have you wished that the rival standing between you and your goal could be removed from the competition? Medea never hesitated, and didn't pull her punches. Her rivals were eliminated – permanently and sometimes without leaving enough enough bits for a proper burial. Kids getting in the way? No kids, no problem.

On the other hand, for issues with a spouse, casual murder is not enough. Here one needs a carefully constructed plot intended to cause maximum psychological damage along with maximum bloodshed. Once again Medea delivers, with literal overkill, but nevertheless manages to portray herself as the anguished victim. In short, there's something liberating about Medea – she does all the things that we wouldn't, because we are too decent, too civilized and frankly, too sane - but nevertheless on occasion we have wanted to.

Another reason why we are able to sympathize with this repeat murderer is because storytelling was much more sophisticated two thousand years ago. In the modern era, many of the stories we see in the cinema or on TV are essentially morality tales. The protagonist is the hero, the antagonist is the villain. The hero is not just good, but wholly good, with character flaws limited to a few amusing quirks. Any hero who falls below this saintly standard is immediately dubbed an 'anti-hero'.

Conversely the modern villain is bad, and totally bad. In fact movie aficionados look for the 'kick the dog' moment when the villain does something gratuitously nasty just to show us that he is irredeemably evil and deserves the grisly fate which will inevitably befall him. Thus – apart from some deliberately contrarian exceptions – most of today's productions aim at providing the audience with 'teachable moments'. We are supposed leave a modern action movie knowing that good will triumph over evil and that our heroes are unconditionally on the 'right' side of every aspect of the modern culture wars.

Greek myth is refreshingly free from such tropes. The objective of a Greek myth is to entertain, not to educate. Rather than portray reality as it should be, Greek myth explains the world as it is. Good does not always triumph over evil - not least because it's hard to work out who is good and who is evil. Instead the characters are just people, some more unpleasant than others, but each with their own motivation for acting in a manner that that seems right to them. In Homer's *Iliad* one can cheer for either the Greeks or the Trojans without feeling morally compromised by the choice and be all the more pleased or shocked when characters do a good or bad thing because they are not forced to do so by the story-teller's moral straitjacket.

So Medea, for all her murderous traits, is more real for us than many a modern action hero. Being real she is a more relatable character – a hero, if you like, albeit one whose moral compass points firmly south. As to the question of whether Medea is 'real' in the historical sense, this biography will not attempt to disentangle truth from myth. Instead it presents the known facts about Medea and leaves readers to accept what they will.

Medea seems real is because she – like so many

characters of myth – is the archetypal figure upon whom many characters of later fiction have been constructed. These archetypes work because they are based upon the way that real people think and behave. We live three thousand years from Medea's day and in a very different culture, yet reading her story we feel that we know her. We may not like her or sympathize with what she has done, but we understand why she did it.

Another positive aspect of Medea is that she has what is today called 'agency'. Rather than she being a victim of circumstance, circumstance is generally a victim of Medea. When we first encounter our protagonist she is living in a backwater that is not only a dead end, but a dead end where her unpleasant father keeps piling up the corpses. Medea wastes no time sitting at the window cursing fate while staring yearningly at unattainable horizons. Instead she spends her days equipping herself with the skills to cope with the outside world that she never doubts she will get to.

When the chance for departure arrives she seizes it with both hands and a trusty dagger. Having decided that she will leave home, Medea unflinchingly does whatever it takes – and leaves the air behind her black with the smoke from burning bridges. Thereafter, whether her decisions are right or wrong, Medea acts decisively. However discomfiting – or even lethal – this may be for those in the immediate vicinity, those of us watching from the safety of the audience know that it is going to be gruesome and horrible - but fascinating.

Medea, with streaming hair, circled the burning altars and dipped many-branched torches into the black ditches filled with blood, and once they were darkened, she lit the torches at the twin altars. Three times with fire, three times with water, three times with sulphur, she performed the rite of purification. Thus, and with a thousand other nameless things, the barbarian witch pursued her greater than mortal purpose. Then seeing all was prepared, Medea unsheathed her blade and cut the old man's throat.

Extracts from *The Rejuvenation of Aeson,* Ovid *Metamorphoses* Bk VII:234-293

Chapter 1

Searching for Medea
The Land and People of Colchis

In 66 BC, many centuries after the story of Medea had passed into legend, the Roman general Gnaeus Pompey decided to visit Colchis, the fabled land of Medea's birth. Pompey's excuse for doing so was because he was ostensibly in pursuit of Mithridates, the king of Pontus in Anatolia, and at this time Mithridates was losing his war with Rome and was retreating through the eastern shores of the Euxine (which today we call the Black Sea).

Really though, Pompey was just indulging in a spot of tourism to relax after a hard campaign. The historian Appian admits that Pompey never really expected Mithridates to make it as far as Colchis, yet alone through that wild and haunted land. (Appian *Mith.* 12.25) For contemporary Greeks and Romans the lands on the further shores of the Euxine were the Wild East – a land rich in gold and natural resources inaccessible because of the rugged terrain and the hostility of the native tribes.

The Colchis that Pompey wanted to see was a dark and deadly land, full of magic, witchcraft and strange beasts. When Horace - a poet of the Augustan era - wanted to describe someone as nastily evil, he reckons such a man would break his own father's neck, murder his guests and 'dabble in Colchian poisons'. (*Carmina*

2.13) Propertius, a near-contemporary of Horace, agrees. 'Magic plants are worth nothing here, nor a Colchian witch of night, nor herbs distilled ... it's a dark path by which many evils come.' (*Elegies* 2.4)

Some Colchian plants deserve their fearsome reputation, such as *Colchicum autumnale* a late blooming plant with beautiful crocus-like flowers. All parts of the plant are highly toxic and there is currently no known antidote for colchicine poisoning. The flowers are reddish-orange, and according to Greek myth there is a particular reason for this – to which we shall come in the next chapter.

In historical times the historian, geographer, ethnologist and narrator of fantastical travellers tales, Herodotus of Halicarnassus, described the Colchians as being so dark-skinned that he reckoned that they were related to the Egyptians. This claim he supported by the fact that like the Egyptians, the Colchians practised circumcision and also like the Egyptians, they produced excellent cloth – cloth and gold being the main non-lethal exports of the region. Herodotus (*Hist* 7.79) also describes Colchian warriors as having wooden helmets, small shields of raw ox-hide, short spears and also swords – probably of the *falcata* type.

Against this hypothesis is the odd and very un-Egyptian burial practice described by Apollonius Rhodius who tells us that dead Colchian males were wrapped in animal skins and hung from the trees for scavenging beasts to consume. Women were buried normally (by our standards, anyway) while the idea of contaminating the sacredness of fire with a human corpse appalled the Colchians – a trait they shared with several religions to their east but very much in contrast with the prevailing Greek practice of cremation.

This reverence for fire might have come from Persia which always had some cultural influence. Indeed, according to Herodotus Colchis was at the northern extremity of the later Persian empire of Cyrus the Great. If so the country had attained independence by the time the soldier and writer Xenophon visited the country as part of the famous March of the Ten Thousand in 400 BC. (When a Greek army was stranded in Persia and made an epic trek through hostile country to the sea.) As Xenophon's army discovered, everything in Colchis had to be handled with care.

There were numerous swarms in bees in the area. Those of the men who ate the honey became demented and suffered from vomiting, and diarrhoea as well. Even those who had eaten just a bit were unable to stand on their feet, as though raving drunk . Meanwhile those who had eaten a lot were like madmen, and in some cases, dying madmen. ... Yet no-one did die and the next day, about twenty-four hours after they had eaten the honey, they came to their senses as though they had been drugged and in three or four days they were again fit for action.

Xenophon, *Anabasis* 4.8.20ff

The Greek army had sampled 'mad honey' a mind-bending neurotoxin produced by bees from the nectar of a few types of rhododendron, one of which (naturally) is native to Colchis. The Colchian natives, who were none too keen on Pompey's visit of 66 BC used the same honey to great effect, leaving honeycombs where the Romans could find them and slaughtering the drugged legionaries while they were helpless.

Pompey, like Xenophon before him, was able to obtain some relief for his soldiers from Greek colonies which appeared on the coast of Colchis in the Classical Era. We find a brief description of these cities in the works of Pseudo-Scylax, who wrote up the notes of a sixth-century explorer of that name. It is from Scylax that we get one of the earliest mentions of Medea's origins.

Next we come to the nation of the Kolchoi, the [Greek] cities of Dioskourias and Tyenoson, and the Gyenos and Xerobios rivers. From Phasis, a Hellenic city, it is 180 stades sailing upriver to Aia, the barbarian city where Medeia came from. Here is the River Ris, the Pirates' river, and the Apsaros river.

Pseudo-Scylax 81

From Scylax, Strabo and other ancient geographers we are able to assemble a picture of the land of Medea's birth. Basically Colchis is that part of the modern state of Georgia which is wrapped around the eastern bay of the Black Sea between the greater and lesser Caucasus mountain chains. The climate is mild to humid and enough rain falls to support several temperate rainforests. The landscape is rugged and dominated by chains of mountains and rivers flowing east to west, occasionally ending in marshes as they reach the sea.

Millet was the main agricultural crop. The lush

meadows produced abundant pasturage for flocks of cattle and sheep, while Colchian horses later came to be praised throughout the Graeco-Roman world. An interesting aspect of the landscape is that it is extremely ancient – being situated between two mountain ranges running east-to-west sheltered Colchis from the glaciation which devastated much of Europe during the last ice age. Consequently Colchis has a large number of relict plants – plants made extinct elsewhere in Europe and a great help to the pharmacopoeia of Medea.

The main river is the Rioni, which was known to the ancient Greeks as the Phasis – from where we get the name of the pheasant (*phasianae aves* – the 'Phasian bird') which by some accounts was introduced to the rest of Europe by Jason and the returning Argonauts - about whom (much) more later. Upstream of the Rioni, shortly after the river branches northward, we come to the city of Cytaesis standing between a mountain massif and the west bank of the river. This city also is given as the place of origin for Medea.

That we have two cities, Aia and Cytaesis both given as Medea's origin town is unremarkable even if we discount the vagaries of myth. Medea after all was the daughter of a king and it was not unusual for ancient monarchs to shift their place of residence according to circumstance, or even according to the season. Since both cities are located on the same river, transferring the king and his court would be merely a matter of loading everything on barges and a few days travel. (Although there might have been a degree of portage required – the River Phasis had a few rough spots. Nevertheless the river was navigable to the extent that tourists can enjoy river tours there today.)

Colchis was at the very edge of the known world. Socrates (in Plato *Phaeto* 109) defines its limits thus, *'I believe that the earth is very large and that we who dwell between the Pillars of Hercules* [the Strait of Gibraltar] *and the River Phasis live in a small part of it ...'*

Another aspect of the River Phasis that is very relevant to our story is that the river ran over several gold-bearing lodes and in consequence panning for gold was a highly profitable operation for the locals. According to the historian Appian, the locals had figured out an even easier way to extract the golden harvest from the river.

'Some of this gold dust is so fine as to be almost invisible. Nevertheless, the natives harvest this by taking shaggy sheepskin fleeces and laying them so that the water of the river is filtered through them.' (*Mithridatic Wars* 12.25) In other words, if you were an ancient adventurer looking for a Golden Fleece, then Colchis would be an excellent place to look.

It should come as no surprise that the people living there did not think of their land as Colchis – they seem to have thought they were living in Aea. However, foreign visitors have a habit of misnaming a land after the first people whom they encountered there. (Thus the Brittones tribe of Kent gave their name to an entire island and thanks to Christopher Columbus' geographical confusion, native American peoples are called Indians after the people whom the Greeks encountered living on the banks of the river Indus – which is now in Pakistan.) In the same way, the Colchians shared their land with the Zygi, Heniochi, Cercetae and Moschi – and if anything, geographically speaking, Medea was Moschian rather than Colchian. However, the Greeks met the Colchi first, and thereafter the land was for them Colchis – a usage we find as early as in the poems of Pindar in 500 BC.

It is rather typical of those enjoying Graeco-Roman civilization that any culture that did not share their common heritage was assumed to have no culture at all. Modern archaeology has been chipping away at the dark, wild and romantic but deadly portrait of Colchis so beloved of classical writers. For example relatively sophisticated bronze implements have been discovered which indicate that Colchis was at a comparable level of civilization with Greece at the end of the first millennium BC. (c.f. N. Rezesidze *et al.* 'Prehistoric metallurgy in mountainous Colchis (Lechkhumi)' *Bulletin of the Georgian National Academy of Sciences* 12(1):183-187 January 2018)

There are also references to a people who seem remarkably like the Colchians in texts from the civilization of ancient Uruatu. Also Pliny the Elder believed that at some unidentified place Colchis clashed with the Egyptian Pharaoh Sesostris in around 1950 BC (Pliny *NH* 33.15). Colchis came out on top, which, given Pompey's experience, is not improbable. We have to assume that. rather than a poisonous mist-shrouded backwater, the Colchis of Medea was actually a well-developed state by contemporary standards, and exotic to the myth-makers of ancient Greece only by reason of its remoteness.

THE LAND AND PEOPLE OF COLCHIS

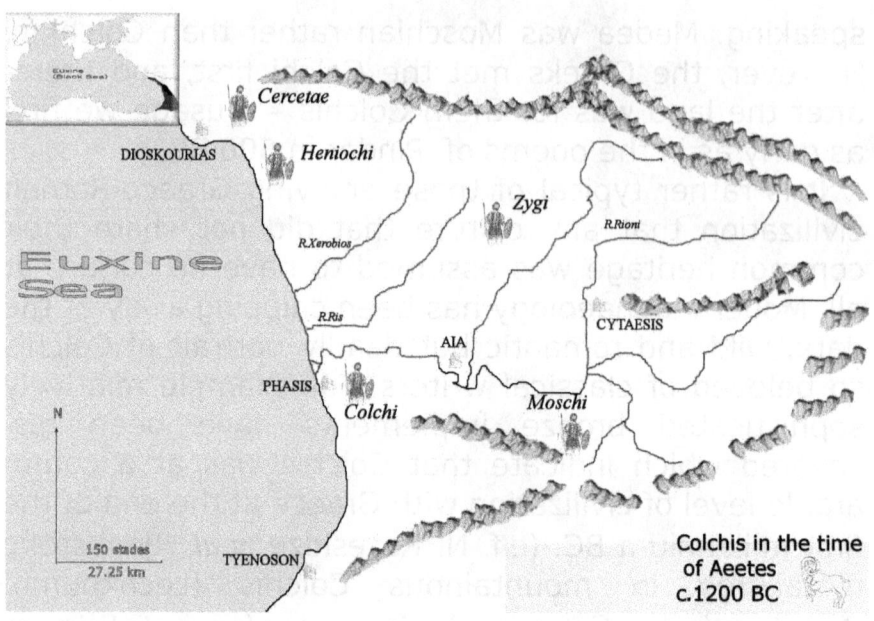

Colchis in the time of Aeetes c.1200 BC

Colchis in myth

Before Jason came to the place with his intrepid Argonauts, Colchis had already seen several major and minor characters from Greek mythology. Perhaps the most famous of these was Prometheus, who was an unhappy permanent guest somewhere in the high Caucasus mountains. Prometheus was not there voluntarily but because he was being gruesomely punished by Zeus, king of the gods. While most religions rather egotistically assume that humanity was created by their supreme being, Greek myth assigned the creation of humanity to Prometheus, who was not the supreme god, nor even one of the twelve Olympians of the later pantheon. He was merely one of the lesser Titans – previously on a par with Atlas, though with less of the world on his shoulders.

Prometheus had been a firm supporter of Zeus in the early days of creation and as a result Zeus was prepared to give Prometheus the benefit of his very substantial - and possibly well-justified – doubt that the creation of humanity was a good idea. Allowed to get on with his pet project, Prometheus set about crafting the first humans from clay and then watched their development with benevolent interest.

It soon became apparent that humans would not rise much above the level of the beasts because Zeus was determined to keep certain essential discoveries out of their hands. Chief among these was the discovery of fire and its many uses. Prometheus was equally determined to overcome this divine technological sanction and when persuasion failed, he simply stole fire from heaven and taught humans how to use it.

The problem with this idea was that eventually Zeus looked down from his home on Mt Olympus and saw the dark earth speckled with the fires of mortals. He knew immediately what had happened and his wrath was terrible.

Quick-witted Prometheus was inescapably bound with cruel chains and Zeus transfixed him with a spear through his abdomen. Then he unleashed a long-winged eagle which came every day to eat the immortal liver; but by night the liver grew to its original size only for the long-winged bird to devour it again the next day.

Hesiod, *Theogony* 520ff

THE LAND AND PEOPLE OF COLCHIS

The place where Prometheus was bound had to be carefully chosen. Greek mythologers could not select a spot which was too convenient, nor yet one so far away that rescue was totally impossible. The obvious location was amid the peaks of those rugged mountains at the very edge of the known world – what today we call the Caucasus mountains of Georgia.

The eagle flew away after each day's meal with blood from the liver of its victim dripping from its beak – blood which was as reddish-orange as the forbidden flames which mankind was now using. Where those drops fell, the earth of Colchis brought forth *Colchicum autumnale*, the beautiful but lethal crocus which formed part of Medea's collection of potions. The Roman poet Valerius Flaccus gives his lurid explanation here -

That Caucasian herb, more potent than any other, created by blood splattered from the liver of Prometheus ... nurtured in snow and bone-chilling frosts when the eagle is gorged upon flesh and gore from his open beak sprinkles the cliffs. Ignorant of the weariness of life that flower stands, immortally fresh against the thunderbolt, its leaves unwithered by lightning.

Hecate, wielding a blade hardened in the Stygian spring, first ripped out the strong stalk from the rocks and showed the plant to her handmaid [i.e. Medea]. *Then she, when Phoebe* [the Moon] *had risen for the tenth time, reaped her harvest from the mountain-side in her mad fury.*

Valerius Flaccus, *Argonautica* 7. 352 ff

Not to leave readers in suspense, Prometheus was eventually rescued – and that rescue was indirectly due to the efforts of Jason and his Argonauts. However, to give the details now would be to get ahead of our story.

At this time Colchis was ruled by a king called Aeëtes. While Aeëtes himself is unknown to all but aficionados of esoteric mythology, the family of Aeëtes contains several well-known figures. The father of Aeëtes was well known for his sunny disposition, but the children of Helios had a somewhat darker character, a family trait which came completely to the fore in the grandchildren of the Sun God, characters who included Medea and the witch-goddess Hecate. The sisters of Aeëtes were also of a magical disposition.

One sister, Pasiphae, became the wife of King Minos of Crete. In a world where male infidelity was the norm Pasiphae kept her husband faithful by gruesomely killing his lovers. Pasiphae's magical formula was a potion which she secretly fed to her husband that caused him to ejaculate spiders and scorpions instead of semen. The fact that Minos was king and those unfortunate women whom he chose to seduce had little choice but to accept his advances did not greatly matter to Pasiphae.

Therefore one has little sympathy when – for reasons we need not go into here – the god Poseidon afflicted her with a perverted lust for a magnificent bull in her husband's possession. In due course Pasiphae gave birth to a monstrous child who was half-man and half-bull – a birth which means that Medea and the Minotaur were cousins – an example of the fact that all of the Greek myths are closely intertwined.

Another of Medea's aunts well-known to posterity is the witch Circe. That is, if we accept the tradition that she was also a child of the sun-god Helios. By another tradition Circe was even more closely related to Medea, being the child of an incestuous relationship between Hecate and Aeëtes. It is certainly true that Hecate was a regular visitor to Colchis, as it is generally agreed that it was she who taught her young cousin Medea the dark arts of spells and potions.

Aunt or step-sister, Circe also possessed that same mean streak that afflicted the other descendants of Helios. When she decided that she fancied an Italian king called Picus that king's refusal of her advances infuriated Circe so much that she turned him into the first woodpecker. (A species still known today by the scientific name of Picidae.) Picus got off lightly.

Consider a handsome fisherman called Glaucus who called upon Circe to help his unsuccessful wooing of a maiden called Scylla. Circe replied

Do you doubt that you are attractive? I am a goddess, daughter of shining Helios, mistress of spells and potions. Yet I promise to be yours. Reject the person who has rejected you, return my affection and the one act will repay you twice.

Ovid, Metamorphoses 14.1

Rejected by Glaucus, Circe responded by picking up some of Hecate's more noxious spells and herbs and dropped the poisonous mixture into a seaside pool where the fair Scylla bathed. Scylla was immediately transformed into a monstrous creature who became a terror to navigation in the narrow strait between Italy and Sicily.

MEDEA, QUEEN OF WITCHES

In her hatred of Circe, she robbed Ulysses of his crewmen. Later she would have destroyed the Trojan ships [of Aeneas] had she had not been transformed into a rock, one that is visible even now and is still feared by sailors. (ibid.)

Circe's big moment in mythology came when she transformed the crewmen of Odysseus/Ulysses into swine. This was far from unprecedented as she had populated the lonely island where she dwelt with the transformed bodies of seamen unfortunate enough to be lured to the shores of her island. Odysseus was protected from Circe's charms by Hermes, though some of Circe's other charms were more effective. She and Odysseus became lovers and he dallied on the island for a year before taking to sea again with his restored crew who promptly became victims of the enraged Scylla.

We shall come later to Medea's uncle, but for now it shall suffice that his name was Perses which means 'The Destroyer' - though fortunately Perses started off far enough to the east of the Mediterranean world for Medea and her immediate family to be out of his blast radius.

Aeëtes, the father of Medea, was a more mild character, though such things were literally relative given the disposition of the rest of the family. True, he succumbed to the occasional homicidal impulse and was lethally xenophobic toward any strangers arriving on the shores of Colchis, but at least he refrained from murder by exotic spells or potions. Various names are suggested for his consort but it seems she was a sea-nymph of some description whom Aeëtes met when he arrived in Colchis from Corinth. Why Aeëtes chose to become ruler of this remote kingdom is unknown, though it has been suggested he was pressured by Hermes to cede his position in Corinth to that god's son.

Medea therefore grew up in wild Colchis, perhaps dreaming of the more settled lands of central Greece, inspired by tales told by her parents. We know she had an older sister called Chalciope and possibly another called Iophossa, and a younger brother called Absyrtus upon whom – rather to Medea's annoyance – both her parents doted. Medea herself, from the little we know, was a solitary and reclusive child. Her closest friendship was with her older cousin Hecate and the times between Hecate's visits were spent roaming the Colchian hills in search of rare and dangerous herbs and in trying out the different magics which Hecate had taught her.

Into the sheltered existence in the secluded kingdom of Medea's family the arrival of a series of strangers managed to turn everyone's life upside down – to the extent where one wonders if Aeëtes did not have a point when he executed newcomers on arrival.

The first of these disruptive strangers came from the south, from Boeotia in central Greece, in the wide plain just across the mountains to the west of Attica. Boeotia was the home of Athamas a king who loved well but not at all wisely. Athamas was the nephew of Aeëtes, being the son of Aeolus, keeper of the winds. Because wind and clouds make a natural pair, Athamas got his romantic life off to a good start by marrying Nephele, the goddess of the clouds. The pair had two children, Helle – a girl, and Phrixus, a boy.

Regrettably, Athamas tired of his marriage and divorced gentle Nephele to marry Ino, daughter of the hero Cadmus, the man who founded the city of Thebes. Ino later raised the child of her deceased sister Semele and that child grew up to become the wine-god Dionysus. (Because all of Greek myth is interconnected it is hard to tell one story without mentioning others.) While a loving aunt to the young Dionysus, Ino was also the stepmother of Helle and Phrixus – and in defiance of the fact that there were and are an abundance of loving stepmothers both in the classical world and today – convention insisted that when it came to her husband's first offspring a stepmother had to be irredeemably evil.

Therefore Ino dutifully came up with a plan to dispose of her step-children – a plan so convoluted and baroque that it should have fallen apart in half-a dozen ways before it ever got off the ground. First Ino got hold of the entire stock of seed corn in Boeotia and gently roasted it to render the corn infertile. When in due course the farmers sowed their seed and nothing grew in the fields, Ino suggested that the people consult an oracle to discover how they could restore life to the fields. Messengers were sent out at once, but they already knew the reply that they would bring back because Ino had purchased their loyalty. She had also coached them to report that nothing would satisfy the angry gods but the sacrifice of Helle and Phrixus.

In due course the sacrifice was prepared, but naturally any sacrifice to the gods was bound to attract the attention of the gods, especially when the children of a goddess were to be sacrificed. As a result Nephele was alerted to the danger facing her children and sent a golden ram to the rescue. Exactly how this rescue was effected we do not know, although over the centuries narrators of the tale decided that a galloping sheep lacked a certain element of drama. Since the fact that the rescuing beast was a ram is essential to later developments, there could be no changing of the species to something more suitable, such as a dragon. Instead the best that could be done was to make the creature airborne. So we must imagine this ram swooping from the heavens, loading the hapless teenagers on to its back and taking off again like a golden comet.

Nephele had instructed the ram to take her children to safety at the ends of the earth, and had presumably cleared the ram for landing at that location - namely the land of Colchis. Clearance was necessary because, as previously mentioned, Aeëtes took dim view of visitors to his kingdom and tended to slaughter them on arrival. (An oracle had warned him that he would lose his kingdom and possibly his life to a stranger from abroad.) However it may have also helped Nephele to arrange a more hospitable reception for her children because Aeëtes was brother to Aeolus. That is, assuming this Aeolus was the wind-god (there are three Aeoli in the myths and very hard to separate from one another) then the children were his nephew and niece in the paternal line.

Sadly Helle did not survive her flight. As the ram was crossing from Europe to Asia Helle fell off the animal's back, and either drowned (if the ram was swimming) or died on impact with the sea after falling from a great height (assuming a ramjet). Her tragic death gave her name greater fame than that of her brother

Phrixus because the sea into which Helle fell became and has remained the Hellespont, the 'Sea of Helle'.

Phrixus landed safely in Colchis and was warmly welcomed by the king who gave the young prince the hand of one of his daughters in marriage. In return Phrixus, as instructed by Nephele, sacrificed the ram – either to Mars (in the Roman version) or to Zeus (in the Greek telling). In either case, the fleece of the ram was shorn and immediately became a symbol of kingship - a symbol which endures in heraldry today. To make sure that this golden fleece was secure, it was hung on a tree in a grove sacred to Ares which stood on the other side of the river Phasis to the royal capital of Aea. As an additional precaution an unsleeping dragon was posted to keep watch over the treasure. If being sacrificed seems a poor reward for the gallant ram, in this case the beast literally did get its reward in heaven – or at least in the heavens – from where it now looks down upon mortals as the constellation of Aries.

Phrixus and his princess bride had three children and for a while it seemed as though everyone was set to live happily ever after. (Apart from the murderous step-mother Ino who threw herself into the sea after being cursed by a vengeful Nephele.) Sadly the oracle which had warned Aeëtes of the threat to his life now added an extra detail – the stranger from overseas who would threaten his kingship would be a relative. The king put two and two together to make five and immediately had the unfortunate Phrixus assassinated.

The children of Phrixus would have been added to the casualties but fortunately they were able to escape to safety. This was thanks to their mother's teenage sister who had taken a shine to the children. This teenage aunt was Medea, who later named one of her son Argus after the oldest of her nephews.

As Aeëtes quickly discovered, he had killed the wrong man. Phrixus was innocent – the true villain was the king's estranged brother Perses who suddenly launched a bid to take over Colchis. Fortunately Aeëtes had in his possession that sacred symbol of kingship, the Golden Fleece, although Perses might legitimately argue that by taking the life of Phrixus, Aeëtes had lost his legitimate claim to that possession. A civil war was imminent and may well have actually started, so it was very unfortunate that this should be the moment when Jason of Iolcus and a boatload of Greek heroes turned up in Colchis to say that actually, the Fleece should be going home with them.

MEDEA, QUEEN OF WITCHES

Roman fresco showing the moment Helle falls from the Golden Ram

Chapter 2

Arrival of a Flawed Hero
Jason and the Voyage of the *Argo*

One of the most enjoyable features of Greek myth is that events seldom happened 'Once upon a time in a faraway country'. Instead, for example, one can even today enjoy a beaker of wine in the town of Nemea, as Hercules probably did after slaying the Nemean Lion. We can wander over the site of Troy speculating where exactly Achilles was standing when he was struck by that fatal arrow. So it is with Jason of Iolcus. Iolcus is a very real place. Anyone wanting to visit can travel to that pleasant little town overlooking a bay on the coast of Thessaly in north-east Greece and study the harbour from which our hero set out on his epic voyage.

In the Heroic Age of early Greece Iolcus, like contemporary Colchis, was suffering from internal strife as the result of a dynastic dispute. The 'king' of Iolcus was one Aeson, who had a half-brother Pelias who was determined to become ruler of all of Thessaly – including the small part of Thessaly ruled by Aeson. There followed a short but brutal palace coup which resulted in Aeson being forced from power, though apparently Pelias allowed him to remain alive to appease the people of Iolcus.

While Pelias kept Aeson in Iolcus, he had no intention of allowing the family line to continue, and this became an issue when Aeson's wife discovered that she was pregnant. By some accounts Aeson was imprisoned in a cave into which the wife had smuggled herself for a secret tryst. The identity of this lady is disputed, but one possibility that she was a descendant of Hermes called Alcimede. If this was the case, the lady apparently inherited some of the cunning of her divine ancestor for when the time came for her to give birth she ensured that her ladies-in-waiting were gathered close around the bed.

When the baby was born the women raised a loud cry of lamentation announcing for all to hear that the child was stillborn. These cries of grief also conveniently hid the cries of a lusty young baby boy, who was in fact very much alive. Alcimede had already arranged for the child to be smuggled from the house to be raised by the centaur Chiron.

As centaurs go, Chiron was an exceptional character. Most centaurs were born from the lust of a disreputable character called Axion and they combined his immoral lack of impulse control with an inability to handle even a sniff of wine. However Chiron was literally a different breed. The standard centaur had a human torso growing out from a horse's neck, but Chiron had simply a horse's body growing from where a human's buttocks would ordinarily be. Chiron was the archetypal old, wise educator of heroes, and his alumni included Theseus, Hercules, the wine-god Dionysus, the healing god Aesculapius, and the Gemini twins Castor and Pollux. It was worth studying with Chiron because he not only was able to simultaneously educate the Greek Achilles and the Trojan Aeneas, but to do so after other myths report that he had already died (giving up his immortality after being shot by a careless arrow from the bow of Hercules). Such mastery over space, time and death itself would definitely make him a highly desirable teacher.

The Heroic Jason of Iolcus

While Jason was growing up Pelias was running into difficulties siring an heir, which made him even more paranoid about the family of his deposed half-brother Aeson. Eventually the uneasy king decided to consult an oracle, where he was informed that his rule would be safe - unless he failed to deal with the threat of the 'man with one sandal'. Had Pelias been a more religious man he might have wondered why the oracle was being so helpful. In fact the oracle was being helpful precisely because Pelias was not a religious man, and the goddess Hera was annoyed that he had neglected his sacrifices. In giving the answer it did, the oracle was setting Pelias up for a fall.

That fall came about as Pelias was preparing athletes to represent Thessaly in the next Olympics. A young man 'eager to do some great deed' - says the poet Valerius Flaccus - arrived at his court, limping slightly because he had lost one of his sandals. This happened because he had helped an old lady across a flooded river, and that lady had somehow managed to detach his footwear – no difficult feat because that old woman was in fact the goddess Hera in disguise.

An agitated Pelias confronted his nemesis and Jason, deciding he had nothing left to lose, revealed himself as the son of Aeson and the rightful heir to the throne of Iolcus. This, as Pelias pointed out, meant that he and Jason had been decreed by destiny to be mortal enemies. So, inquired Pelias, what would Jason do if he was in Pelias' shoes and Pelias in Jason's single sandal? As a young man with immortal fame at the forefront of his mind, Jason had his answer at the ready. 'I would send myself to retrieve the Golden Fleece from Colchis', he answered without hesitation.

So the deal was made. Jason would set off on his suicide mission and if by any improbable chance he returned with the Fleece – the symbol of kingship, it will be recalled – Pelias would abandon the throne which he had usurped. Unfortunately for him, Pelias lacked the practice of King Eurysthenes who was at this time setting various even more suicidally difficult labours for Hercules. So Pelias in his deal with Jason neglected to add the sub-clause which Eurysthenes had carefully inserted – that the hero was to perform his task alone and unaided.

Jason proceeded to drive a four-horse chariot through that loophole and set about gathering the most formidable band of heroes ever to assemble in one place prior to the Trojan war. The full list, for those who wish to consult it, can be found in the *Argonautica* of Apollonius Rhodius bk 1.18ff.

First up – and doubtless to his father's very great annoyance – was one Acastus of Iolcus, the son of King Pelias himself. Another early volunteer was Argus, a ship-builder of great repute who immediately set about crafting for Jason a ship suitable for the challenges of their seaborne mission. A family connection with Colchis came from Deucalion, son of Pasiphae of Crete and therefore the cousin of Medea. Other demi-divines flocked to join the crew, including the offspring of Zeus, Poseidon, Hermes, Helios and Dionysus.

Foremost of the notable heroes assembled was mighty Hercules himself, something about which Jason definitely had ambiguous feelings. On the one hand having a hero like Hercules along was as near as a guarantee of success as the mission could be given. On the other hand, Jason was on this mission for the glory and any adventure involving Hercules tended to become the Adventure of Hercules and his Sidekicks – and thanks to the enmity of Hera who hated Hercules, many of these sidekicks became collateral fatalities before the end of any given saga. Hercules also did not play well with others, having an ego as large as his muscles. Furthermore another of the crew was the famed musician Orpheus and he probably held something of a grudge against Hercules, who had killed his brother Linus in a tragic lyre accident. (It's a long story.)

So it was remarkable that before joining the crew Hercules gave a modest little speech announcing that he intended to take a back seat on this mission, subordinate himself to Jason and only step up if really needed.

Then there were Peleus (later to be the father of Achilles), and the Gemini – the twin sons of Zeus called Castor and Pollux who were born of the Spartan queen Leda at the same time as their more famous sister Helen of Troy. Another whom Jason considered but ultimately rejected was the beautiful Atalanta, whose name means 'of the same weight ', in that she packed as much heft as her heroic male counterparts. Certainly Atalanta was well-qualified as a hero. Indeed, as the famed slayer of the dreaded Calydonian Boar, she was better qualified than most. However, as well as being beautiful Atalanta was a virgin and very serious about remaining so – to the point where she had already slain a pair of suitors who became too insistent on removing that status. Putting this maiden in the close confines of a boatload of over-sexed heroes was a prospect which caused Jason to shudder gently and strike Atalanta's name from the list of potential recruits.

Even without Atalanta, this crew of some 50-70 heroes (plus Hercules) were a formidable bunch, and they needed a vessel to match. After all, this was a ship which had to carry the crew to the ends of the known earth. The ship was to be 'swift' which the writer Diodorus Siculus assures us is what 'argo' means, though Cicero thought the ship's name was derived from 'Argives' which was a contemporary alternative name for the Greeks. Others reckon the name came from that shipwright who, like the son of Phrixus (and many others) was named Argus.

Athena and Hera pooled their efforts to aid Argus in the construction of the vessel. Athena, as the goddess of wisdom, also set about teaching the helmsman his craft and showed the others how to properly rig the sail of their extraordinary vessel. The prow of the ship was crafted by oak obtained through a special dispensation from the sacred grove of Dodona, where Zeus himself pronounced oracles through the whispering of the wind in the leaves. The oak from Dodona retained the power of speech, and a degree of oracular ability, and is thus the only craft known that could discuss matters of course and sailing with the captain and steersman.

We are told that the ship was able to carry supplies for around two weeks before the heroes had to restock, yet was light enough to be carried over land by the crew, as they once had to do for twelve days straight because of mythological complications.

After these drawn-out and meticulous preparations, Jason had finer a ship and crew than had ever before been assembled. The night before their departure the crew partied on the beach, sacrificed to the gods, got drunk and quarrelled, all as Greek heroes should. The unusual aspect of their departure came the next morning, 'when gleaming dawn with bright eyes beheld the lofty peaks of Pelion' says the poet who tells this tale. That is when the good ship *Argo* itself, impatient to be off, started to yell at the crew to get their lazy carcasses aboard. The hungover heroes duly shambled up the gangplank while Jason - as Greek lads of any era are obliged to do – stoically endured a tearful farewell from his mother. Then with the entire population of Iolcus in attendance, plus sightseers from further afield, the dauntless band set off with adventure, danger and romance waiting just beyond the horizon.

The first hazard which the crew encountered on the way to Colchis was not adventure or danger, but romance. Cupid came close to taking the expedition on to the rocks before the *Argo* had got further than the isle of Lemnos, a few days sailing out of Thessaly. At the time the island was suffering from the results of a severe bout of misandry, for the native men had gone slave-raiding in Thrace and had brought home a large number of female captives whom they preferred to their own womenfolk. The ladies of Lemnos did not take rejection well, and in a well-synchronized massacre they disposed of their husbands by dagger, poison and by casting them out to sea. Then, deciding there was no need to stop at half-measures, they went on to kill every other man on the island.

Thereafter their community of widows and spinsters set about learning how to plough, don armour, and do other tasks formerly beyond their domain, but all the while feeling that something was missing from their lives. The nature of that something dawned upon them when a boatload of husky heroes disembarked looking for water and supplies but by no means averse to a bit of companionship. Night followed day and then more nights and days each filled with parties, banquets and merry-making as the Argonauts strove to find new reasons why they should remain for still a few nights more.

As the months slipped by towards the end of the sailing season it fell to Hercules to step up, as he had said he would do in times of emergency. Certainly at this point Jason was of little use. He was as smitten with the queen of Lemnos as his crew were with the other females of the isle. It is not that Hercules had more self-control than the average Greek hero (who basically didn't have any), but at the time Hercules was deeply in lust with a beautiful young crewman called Hylas and was therefore less vulnerable to the delights of heterosexuality than the rest of the crew.

Accordingly Hercules gathered the men together and gave them a sound tongue-lashing. 'What are we doing here, exactly?' he demanded. 'Are we exiled for murder from our native lands? Can we not find wives at home? Did we set out for glory only to end up ploughing the fields of Lemnos? Oh, I get it. You are all hoping that some God will hear your prayers and provide you with a self-propelled fleece that is going to come to you of its own accord. Or do you fancy seeking glory like that fellow who lies in the embrace of the queen seeking to gain fame by single-handedly re-manning the island with boy-children?' (*Argonautica* 853)

The Herculean harangue had its effect, and the chastised crew admitted to themselves that they had dallied on Lemnos for too long. They agreed that they should set sail the moment they succeeded in prising Jason out of the arms of the queen - which was no easy task as the pair had become very close.

A tearful parting followed and then Jason led his men aboard the *Argo* to set sail for their next destination, the island of Electra, there to learn the secret rites that would preserve them from the wrath of the elements while at sea. (Electra was the mother of that Dardanus for whom the Dardanelles are named, and also – through her name, which means 'amber' - the etymological mother of the elemental force of electricity.)

Thereafter the crew passed uneventfully through the Hellespont to sail upon 'the dark and gleaming currents' of the Euxine, today known as the Black Sea, with Colchis waiting on the north-eastern shore. The Argonauts put ashore at the city which was to be named after its first ruler, Cyzicus. The city (now a picturesque ruin upon the north coast of Anatolia) shared the peninsula upon which it stood with a race of six-armed giants. These, deciding that the *Argo* must be loaded with treasure, descended upon ship and city in a homicidal wave. The citizens of Cyzicus and the Argonauts combined forces to fight off the monsters, but thereafter it was mutually agreed that it was probably best if the *Argo* set sail again at once.

This plan was upset by reality, for the *Argo* ran into one of those sudden squalls for which the Black Sea is infamous. After battling ferocious winds all day, the Argonauts were forced back to the beach on Cyzicus from which they had recently embarked. It was now night, and pitch-dark owing to the ongoing storm. Assuming that the monsters had used the weather to mount yet another attack, the people of Cyzicus bravely pulled on their armour and charged the beach where the Argonauts, assuming that they were under attack by the monsters, fought back ferociously.

A bloody, confused and totally pointless battle followed with casualties on both sides. However, the Argonauts were, after all, a boatload of heroes doing what they did best while the Cyzicans were merely enthusiastic amateurs. The Argonauts put them to flight just before dawn revealed whom they had been fighting. Dawn also revealed that king Cyzicus himself lay among the dead, a discovery which drove his distraught wife to suicide. Oddly enough though, this catastrophic incident brought Argonauts and Cyzicans tog-ether in shared grief. This they expressed at funeral games for the deceased before the *Argo* set sail again, this time into dead calm.

These past few days had seen the best and worst of Hercules. As expected. he had mown down the six-armed monsters with ruthless efficiency, but there was a suspicion among the crewmen that the only reason that the monsters were there in the first place was because Hera's hatred for Hercules had inspired the attack. Now, when their ship was becalmed, Hercules grew impatient with the speed at which the heroes were rowing the *Argo* through the waters of the Euxine.

Taking a sighting on a distant island, Hercules ordered the rest of the crew into the bow to hold down the ship while he selected the two strongest oars and powered the *Argo* towards land at hydroplane speed. They had nearly reached the island when one of the oars snapped, causing Hercules to topple backwards into the bilges in a spectacular pratfall. This would have been hilarious if the glare of Hercules had not made it clear that the first hint of a snigger would be followed by sudden death. That afternoon, as they beached their ship on the island, it seems that a common sentiment grew among the crew that while life was easier with Hercules around, it would probably also be a lot shorter.

The lethally irritable Hercules

Hercules and Hylas headed away from the campsite with Hercules muttering something about uprooting a sturdy pine or two that he could fashion into a more suitable set of oars. The pair were away all night and come daybreak Hercules was still no-where to be found. The crew hastily packed their bags and piled aboard ship, assuring each other that evidently some misadventure had befallen the hero. It was terribly sad, and Hercules would be greatly missed, but they had a quest to get on with and they should get on with it sooner than later. A following wind promised fair sailing, so really it was impossible to wait. With such thoughts in mind the heroes set sail as fast as possible before an enraged Hercules could emerge from the trees to find that he had been marooned.

Once safely out to sea the Argonauts had second thoughts. Hercules was famously vindictive and being abandoned on a faraway island was not the sort of inconsiderate behaviour that he took lightly. The crew began debating whether to turn back, with some in favour and 'the sons of Boreas' arguing against it. Jason sat somewhat haplessly as the debate raged about him until one hero came right out and challenged him with it.

'Sitting there comfortably, are you? It has worked out well for you that we decided to leave Hercules behind. You always wanted the glory of this project, and now that he is gone there will be no-one to overshadow your fame should the gods allow us a safe return home. I'm not discussing it any more. I'm going back, preferably without those comrades of yours who helped with this treachery.' (*Argonautica* l.1295)

From there, things might have deteriorated into a full-scale shipboard brawl had not a messenger from the sea-god Nereus suddenly popped his head up alongside the boat. This apparition told the crew that Hercules had been sidetracked because water-nymphs had kidnapped the beautiful Hylas. It was the will of Zeus that the crew should continue without their mighty companion, who was distracted firstly by his search for his lover, and secondly because he still had several of his famous labours to complete.

(Hercules went on to wreak havoc across eastern Anatolia as he made his way overland to Colchis, defeating a variety of enemies, killing the Amazon queen in the course of Labour #9, and allying with the Mysian tribe to conquer Bithynia. He never did meet up again with Jason, though in later years he vindictively took the trouble to track down the sons of Boreas and killed them as they were returning from the games on the island of Temnos.)

For the Argonauts various adventures followed, the most notable of which was a battle with the infamous Harpies who were making life miserable for an ancient but wise seer who lived on an island close to the dread Clashing Rocks which made that part of the sea impossible to shipping. In exchange for Jason and his crew seeing off the Harpies, the seer instructed them how to avoid being ground to paste between the rocks. Armed with this knowledge the team proceeded eastwards, stopping on occasion to pick up survivors of Hercules' land-based rampage and discovering that it was unsafe to land in Amazonian territory as the warrior-women were still somewhat bitter about Hercules' recent visit.

After their hasty departure from the wrath of the Amazons it probably began to dawn upon the Argonauts that Jason, their heroic leader was, well, neither much of a leader nor in fact particularly heroic. Having led the charge into the beds of the Lemnian women, he had been the last to be dragged out of there. Nor had he particularly distinguished himself in the various scraps and skirmishes since. On the issue of whether to abandon Hercules he had simply sat and let the debate rage about him.

While the average testosterone-laden mythological hero was more than ready to take circumstances by the forelock and bend things to his will, Jason was curiously passive. He allowed events to dictate his actions and would meekly step aside whenever one of his crewmen decided to seize the initiative. One might imagine a degree of muttered speculation among the crew as to how Jason would conduct himself when the *Argo* finally arrived in Colchis.

First though, that same aged seer who had instructed the Argonauts how to avoid the Clashing Rocks had also insisted that the crew must on no account leave the Isle of Ares out of their Euxine travels. This occasioned a degree of bewilderment, for the Isle of Ares was inhabited by a particularly nasty type of bird. Like a lethal sort of flying porcupine these birds shook off razor-sharp feathers to impale their victims below. In the end, the Argonauts only fought the birds off by donning armour and clashing swords against their bronze-faced shields to frighten them away.

Once they had beached their ship on that inhospitable shore the reason for the seer's instructions became apparent. The adventurers were met by a bedraggled band of castaways who had recently been shipwrecked on the island. Their leader revealed himself as Argus, the son of Phrixus who had fled Colchis after Aeëtes had mistakenly murdered his father. Jason was delighted to add the refugees to this crew. Given that Phrixus was the original owner of the Golden Fleece, having the son of Phrixus in his retinue certainly added legitimacy to Jason's claim upon the treasured article.

Argus, on the other hand, was less than enthusiastic about returning to Colchis and assured Jason that getting Aeëtes to part with his treasured fleece would be no easy feat.

My friends, should you need me make no mistake, I shall aid you to the best of my ability and hold nothing back. But I dread making this trip. Aeëtes calls himself the son of a God and he is both deadly and ruthless, and furthermore the tribes of Colchis are many and warlike. Indeed Aeëtes alone might contend with Ares himself, so fearsome is his battle-cry and giant strength. And to get the Fleece from him involves another difficult challenge – coiled about the fleece is a huge, unsleeping serpent, an immortal creature conceived by Gaia herself on the slopes of the Caucasus mountains.

Argonautica 1196ff

This little speech rather shook the crew, but Peleus the future father of Achilles rallied the men, assuring them that things would probably not be that bad, and gradually the Argonauts talked themselves into continuing with their mission. An unkind soul might have noted that this was the moment for Jason to step up with some inspiring words, but it seems the crew had given up looking for leadership from that direction.

By now the *Argo* was fast approaching its destination. The Caucasus mountains reared up on the horizon and the day came when the sail of the ship was shaken by the wind from the passage of a gigantic eagle. The crew shuddered as the heights resounded with the agonized screams of Prometheus as the eagle yet again feasted upon the liver of its bound victim.

The crew of the *Argo* were among the last to hear those dreadful shrieks, for Prometheus had been in negotiations with Zeus about regaining his freedom. Prometheus had some powers of prophecy and he had foreseen how one day soon Zeus might be overthrown. The exact details of what happened next were carefully described by the playwright Aeschylus in the fifth century, although the play describing events (*Prometheus Unbound*) was carelessly lost in the centuries thereafter. Lacking the guidance of Aeschylus we are now forced to attempt a reconstruction from the fragments of different myths which remain.

The critical factor may have been the arrival of the hero Peleus off the coast of Colchis. Once the *Argo* came within range, Prometheus was able to foresee that one day Peleus would marry the neriad Thetis. This was important because Zeus was contemplating the seduction of Thetis, and Prometheus knew that any child whom Thetis bore was fated to be greater than his father. A son greater than himself would be a major problem for Zeus who had come to power by overthrowing his own father and was consequently well aware of how things might play out.

Were he properly forewarned, the way out of the problem would be for Zeus to step back and get Thetis married to someone safe in a hurry. It now appeared that Peleus the Argonaut was fated to be the destined bridegroom. All this Prometheus now knew, and he was prepared to disclose this vital information to Zeus in exchange for being freed - and for someone to kill that damned eagle.

As it happened the perfect person to meet both of the conditions proposed by Prometheus was currently present in the Caucasus mountains. This was Hercules, vengefully making his way towards Colchis where he intended to have strong words with Jason and the Argonauts. Instead, thanks to successful negotiations between Zeus and Prometheus, Hercules was diverted from his mission of revenge by his divine father, Zeus.

The hero was ordered to ascend to the peaks and there rip from the rock the chains of adamantine by which Prometheus was bound. Then, when the eagle arrived for his customary dinner, he was met instead by Hercules who made short work of the bird – an event which we may assume that Prometheus observed with considerable satisfaction. Thereafter Prometheus and Hercules settled down for a long talk. All we know or can guess of what happened in this discussion was that Prometheus revealed certain details of the hero's future – information sufficient for Hercules to abandon his intention of travelling to Colchis and instead return to Greece.

(As an aside, Thetis did indeed marry Peleus and bear him a son mightier than his father. While few today have heard of Peleus, his son Achilles still casts a mighty shadow across the landscape of myth.)

Unaware that they had narrowly escaped a grisly confrontation with Hercules, the Argonauts finally reached their destination.

They immediately lowered the yard-arm and stowed the sail below the mast. Then they lowered the mast also so that it lay lengthways [down the ship]. Using oars they powered their ship upriver with the mighty waters surging around the prow. On the left were the towering Caucasus peaks and the city of Aea, on the other the Plain of Ares and his sacred grove where the serpent lay guarding the Fleece which hung from the leafy branches of an oak tree. Then, from a golden goblet, Jason poured a libation of honey and unwatered wine in thanks to Gaia and the gods of Colchis, calling upon them and upon the spirits of deceased heroes, asking them to grant him aid and to look kindly upon his mission.

The the hero Ancaeus spoke up. 'Well we have reached Colchis and rowed up the river Phasis – now it is time to decide whether we are going to try to charm Aeëtes with soft words, or whether we should go directly to the alternative.'

Argonautica 1262ff

They moored the *Argo* in a quiet backwater of the river Phasis, there to debate their next move. Given that the prow of the *Argo* was sentient and quite capable of joining in the discussion, it is increasingly clear that the ship's real figurehead was Jason, who sat back to see what his followers would decide. What neither Jason nor this crew of heroes could have known was that they were not the only ones having this conversation. The fate of the Argonauts and the Golden Fleece - and of Medea - would be decided at quite a higher level.

Chapter 3

Securing the Fleece

As we have already seen, Jason had a powerful patron in Hera, the consort of Zeus. From the start Hera had helped to get Jason to the royal court of Pelias in Iolcus, and she had been instrumental in getting him sent on his current quest. For Hera the original point of Jason's mission was to have him return to Iolcus with the Golden Fleece as proof of his right to the throne. This would cause the downfall of King Pelias, and this for Hera was the object of the exercise. As she explained, 'Pelias is not going to mock me by escaping from a horrible fate – he who never honours me with sacrifices.' As their relationship progressed, Hera had developed a soft spot for Jason, beginning at the moment he had hoisted her on to his muscular shoulders in the belief that he was helping an elderly sandal thief across a fast-flowing river.

Now that the *Argo* was parked alongside the coveted Golden Fleece, Hera sought the wisest way of helping Jason to separate Aeëtes from his treasured possession. Unlike ordinary mortals in need of wisdom Hera had direct access to the personification of wisdom itself, so she pulled Athena aside for a strategy meeting.

The pair agreed that even with his current domestic problems, Aeëtes was still a formidable foe. Moreover, he was also likely to be immune to the 'soft words and persuasion' which Hera felt ought to be tried as a first resort. (*Argonautica* 2.5ff)

Hera (right) and Athena, adapted from a 5th century Greek Vase

Athena admitted that she had considered a number of alternatives but still had not come up with a viable plan. For the moment she was stumped. Therefore the Goddess of Wisdom was possibly slightly miffed when – after the pair had brooded on the situation a while – Hera was the first to come up with a workable idea.

The solution, reckoned the cunning goddess, was love not war. What Jason needed was someone close enough to Aeëtes to influence the king yet also powerful enough to control events unaided. In other words, it was time to bring into play the daughter of Aeëtes – Medea the sorceress. Hera was aware that Medea had already developed powerful magical abilities. Medea had also shown that she was prepared to defy her father when she had arranged the escape of the children of the executed Phrixus - those same children whom Jason had recently picked up after their shipwreck off the Isle of Ares. Medea would be a powerful ally on Jason's side, and the easiest way to recruit the formidable Medea would be to give her powerful motivation to join the cause. And what force is more powerful than love?

So, just as Athena was on hand when Hera went looking for wisdom, when looking for love Hera again went straight to the source – Aphrodite herself. Aphrodite listened sympathetically to Hera's problem. She agreed that should persuasion fail to part Aeëtes from his Fleece then this would be a case best solved by a visit to Medea by her henchboy, Cupid. Neither goddess seems to have considered Medea's feelings in the matter. This shows a certain (not untypical) callousness, for in the ancient world getting struck by Cupid was often considered on par with being struck by the plague.

For a start, Cupid had not one but two sets of arrows with which he created havoc among mortals. Most people know of the gold-tipped arrows which arouse passionate love in those whom the mischievous god has targeted. Less well-known are the lead-tipped arrows which arouse a similar degree of repugnance. On occasion even the gods had suffered when Cupid darted one victim with gold and the intended paramour with lead. Small wonder then, that Cupid was sometimes referred to as the 'Messenger of Pain'. (*Argonautica* 3.275)

SECURING THE FLEECE

This time, with remarkable economy, the Goddesses collectively decided that only Medea need be struck with a gold-tipped arrow. Either Jason would fall in love of his own accord or he would not reciprocate Medea's passion – either outcome was a matter of indifference to the goddesses. It was Medea's performance in helping Jason get the Fleece that counted.

So with Cupid locked and loaded, Hera watched as Jason, armed with no more than a herald's staff, went to the palace of Aeëtes to see if words alone could do the trick. He was unaccompanied by the Argonauts, whom he had persuaded to remain with their ship but he brought with him the children of Phrixus in the hope that their return would at least soften up the mother, who was after all another daughter of Aeëtes.

A thick mist covered the city as Jason made his way to the palace, so when he arrived the hero was rather startled to discover that rather than some rude rustic hold, Aeëtes lived in a veritable citadel with towering walls, elegant gardens, fountains and magnificent royal apartments. It was certainly not the sort of place that could be stormed by fifty crewmen from the *Argo*, though certified heroes were they all. Time then, for Cupid to do his thing.

The demonic little archer was already secreted like an assassin above one of the lintels of the temple where Medea served as a priestess of Hecate. Attracted by the commotion when Jason and the children of Phrixus appeared in the courtyard, Medea stepped out of the temple. At the moment she first set eyes on Jason, Cupid let fly. Medea took an arrow straight to the chest.

MEDEA, QUEEN OF WITCHES

The arrow hit Medea's heart like a flaming torch making it beat fast with sweet agony in her breast, her mind swam, and her soul melted. ... As dry twigs catch fire when heaped about a blazing log and wrap it in flame as though embracing their destroyer, so did love coil about her heart. She kept darting quick, bright glances at Jason while her cheeks alternately flamed red or went deathly pale, mirroring the turmoil of her soul.

Argonautica 3.382ff

Aphrodite's little Archer – Fresco in the villa of the Vetii, Pompeii

Thus, from the casual spite held by Hera against a king whom Medea had never met, began one of the great unrequited love affairs of myth, the echoes of which still resound today. Of course, it is also possible that Hera and Cupid need not have bothered. Medea was a young but extremely powerful sorceress who might well have been feeling herself constrained by the limitations of her father's palace and the isolation of Colchis. Then, like a breath of fresh air, in breezed this handsome hero from the exotic, sophisticated world of central Greece. It was certainly enough to get a maiden's heart pounding even without divine intervention.

Medea also had to face up to the sad fact that hers might also be a very brief romance. There was a good chance that Jason would not even survive dinner with her father once he had raised the subject of taking the Fleece. Indeed, as it turned out, the only thing which saved Jason from getting executed on the spot was that the topic of the Fleece only came up after the first course of dinner had been consumed. Argus, the son of Phrixus, had cunningly kept the conversation on his travails after being shipwrecked upon the island of Ares. Once he had eaten meat and drunk wine at the table of Aeëtes, Jason was officially a guest. It was not just bad manners to kill a guest, doing so also provoked the anger of the god of hospitality - who happened to be Zeus himself.

Therefore, although he was practically choking with fury, Aeëtes had to contain himself. He already had a lively civil war on his hands. He could hardly afford to add the enmity of a boatload of the top heroes of Greece by doing something homicidal to their captain that would also put the Gods firmly against him. Jason had implied that he had divine backing for his quest, so before executing this impertinent stranger it might be an idea to check exactly what that divine protection entailed.

Jason was aware that his request had caused grave offence. He tried to pacify the outraged Aeëtes by offering the services of his collection of heroes as mercenaries who would help Aeëtes with his military endeavours. Instead, Aeëtes proposed something closer to home. The craftsman god Hephaestus had gifted Aeëtes a pair of flame-breathing oxen in the past. Aeëtes was in the habit of using these oxen to plough the field of Ares alongside the sanctuary where the Fleece was kept. All Aeëtes wanted was for Jason to plough and sow that field - and survive.

While the oxen were unreasonably murderous in their own right, they were not the real problem. The sowing was to be performed not with grain but with dragon's teeth - and after the teeth had hit the furrow an armed man would spring up in that place. Aeëtes airily explained that he would then cut down these ferocious warriors and harvest the weapons and armour. It was reasonable enough, he argued, that he should hand over the Fleece to someone who was his equal, but he was not going to give up his prized possession to an inferior. So if Jason would do the day's harvesting for him, he would consider the Argonaut's request for the Fleece.

When the case was presented in this manner, Jason had no choice but to agree to commit what was in all practical terms suicide by oxen. His appetite gone, a despondent Jason left the king's banqueting hall in the company of his retinue. Argus, the son of Phrixus, came out of the hall with him and hastened to give the depressed Jason some advice.

SECURING THE FLEECE

You might not like what I'm going to tell you, but nasty as the situation is, you can't back out. So listen, you've heard me tell of this maiden who uses sorcery as a student of Hecate. Win her over and this trial you face will not be a problem. And you have to win — for I have a feeling that my neck is on the line here also.

Argonautica 3.471

Meanwhile back at the palace, Medea was coming to roughly the same conclusion. Jason was remarkably handsome, he moved with grace and spoke with eloquence, yet he clearly was not up to the task which he had been set. Heart-throb though he may be, come morning Jason was going to be burned alive and his ashes trampled into the mud by the oxen of Aeëtes. Medea felt that at the very least she should go and see Jason and let him know that, while she would much prefer that he escape unharmed, if Jason was fated to be shredded then she at least was going to regret it. But was this the sort of thing a modest maiden should say by way of introducing herself to a potential swain?

Of course, the love-struck Medea knew that she herself could do the task set for Jason, and do it easily, but that was not the point. The task had been given to Jason and he would have to be the one who saw it through or her father would simply rule the whole trial invalid. (The same thought had not occurred to the Argonauts, who were at the same moment arguing with one another about who should do the task once Jason had failed to do it himself.) Under the circumstances, Medea could hardly present herself to a boatload of macho heroes and inform them that actually they were redundant because she, Medea, had developed a crush on their leader and was going to do the job herself. Apart from the outrage of the heroes, what would her sister and family think of her wanton behaviour should she launch herself at the newcomer like that?

They would throw insulting taunts at me and tales of my conduct will spread to every city. My name will be on the lips of every woman of Colchis, passed back and forth as they revile and mock me - the girl who put her very life on the line because of her passion for a stranger. The woman who shamed her parents and home because of her crazed lust. Oh, this infatuation of mine will bring every kind of disgrace.

Argonautica 3.771

So out of maidenly modesty Medea decided not to put herself forward and sat quietly sobbing in her room at the forthcoming termination of her unrequited love affair. She was unaware that aboard the *Argo* the conversation had moved on to an anxious discussion as to how her aid might possibly be recruited. She was also unaware that her sister was in her room with her children scheming how to persuade Medea to help Jason with his challenge. In short, everyone but Aeëtes was feverishly plotting to get Medea to do something they did not realize that she desperately wanted to do.

In the end it was the fate of young Argus and the other children of Phrixus that gave Medea her excuse. Medea's sister came to her room and pleaded with Medea to help Jason, since otherwise she was reasonably sure that Aeëtes intended to kill her children for allying themselves with the Argonauts. This plea gave

Medea a chance to conceal her bounding delight and gravely admit that well, yes, since the lives of her her nephews were at stake perhaps it behooved her to do something, however improper it might seem.

Sister, I shall do this thing because you and your sons are a delight to me. May I never live to see another sunrise if I put anything before the lives of your sons, who are like brothers to me, youthful companions and dear kinsmen.

Argonautica 3.724

Nevertheless, Medea spent a sleepless night going over and over her decision. Because her magical abilities included a degree of premonition, she knew that this was one of the defining moments of her life. She could still abandon Jason to his fate and live out her days quietly in Colchis, eventually to die unknown to any but her immediate family, with the potential of her powers untested. Or she could turn her back upon her father and homeland, accept her destiny and become Medea – that great and fearsome sorceress, as feared for her lethal ruthlessness as for her terrible powers.

When she put it to herself like that, there could be no question as to her choice – she *was* Medea, chosen by Hera to be Jason's companion and frankly, his better half. Henceforth she would be herself and put self-doubt and questioning aside. With the first light of dawn shining into her chamber, Medea dressed in her finest robes and ordered mules harnessed to her chariot. Carefully selecting rare and precious potions from her casket, she prepared to set out with her maidservants for the shrine of Hecate, there to prepare her ingredients.

Colchine, of course, but that vintage of colchine extracted from plants sprung upon the flanks of the Caucausan mountains – a rare species about to become extinct now that Hercules had freed Prometheus. The titan's blood no longer dripped from the beak of the eagle that fed upon him, so no more would that blood cause to grow the crocus-coloured plants with roots like new-cut flesh. Medea had prepared her extract some time ago. In the dark of night she had once made it into an unguent while calling upon the Queen of the Dead herself to assist in the making. Now it was time to put the potion into play.

By leaving the palace Medea made it clear that she had thrown in her lot with the Argonauts. As she rode her chariot through the city not a woman would meet her eyes. Furthermore, the meadow near the shrine of Hecate had been hastily abandoned as soon as her destination had become apparent. By now Medea was past caring. She informed her servants, 'My friends, it seems I have given grave offence now that I have openly sided with the strangers. The whole city is dismayed and none remain of the crowds who usually throng this meadow. Well, to Hades with the lot of them. I have summoned Jason to meet me here, so let us gather what we need and when he arrives, let no-one interfere.'

Jason was indeed on his way, well aware that he was wooing for his life. Hera knew it also and had done her best to cast a glamour on her protege. The sunlight bounced off his perfect cheekbones at the perfect angle, his eyes never looked steelier, nor had his muscles ever rippled more alluringly. As he set off on his mission the hero's companions looked at him in amazement, wondering what had come over him.

And so, never having looked more heroic, our hero strode down the path towards Medea. As the poet put it, 'As Sirius [the star] rises over the sea, bright and beautiful, for all the calamity it will bring to flocks [through drought and summer heat] so did Jason come to her ... and there they met and stood silent as two tall pines together on a mountainside.'

After gazing rapturously into one another's eyes for a while, Jason broke the spell. He appealed for Medea's help, pointing out that not only his life but that of his boatload of heroes now rested in her hands. Should she decide to help the Argonauts, there was a legion of wives, sisters and daughters who would sing her praises throughout Hellas for allowing their menfolk to return home unscathed.

The poet then says that Jason assured Medea that she would become even more famous than Ariadne, the helper-maiden without whose assistance Theseus would have been unable to slay the Minotaur and escape from the labyrinth. This is an odd excursus, firstly because it is wildly anachronistic. Theseus had yet to be born and his meeting with Ariadne on Crete lay some two decades in the future.

Secondly, even if Jason were somehow able to foretell how that particular myth would play out, it was quite certainly a very undiplomatic example to select. As Medea was planning to do, Ariadne was to betray her father, help the hero to complete his mission and then escape with him on his ship. Then, when their boat stopped on the island of Naxos to gather supplies, Ariadne wandered into the woods. She returned to the beach just in time to see the sail of Theseus' boat vanishing over the horizon.

Jason and Medea in a 17th century etching

The story of a hero callously abandoning the woman who had sacrificed everything to help him is a definitely odd example for Jason to bring up just at the time when he was urging Medea to sacrifice everything to

SECURING THE FLEECE

help him. Fortunately, being blind and deaf with passion, Medea barely heard a word Jason was saying. Wordlessly she drew from her girdle the unguent she had prepared for Jason. Indeed she would have drawn her soul from her breast and given him that also, so well had Cupid done his work. The pair stood smiling stupidly at one another for some time before it eventually filtered through Medea's love-addled brain that application of the unguent needed instructions if it was to work properly.

Firstly, Jason was to go to the palace and get his sackful of dragon's teeth for the sowing. However, rather than proceed directly to the field he should put off the job for the next day. Then at midnight he was to go to the river and purify himself in the waters. Then he needed to dig a fire-pit and sacrifice there an ewe in the flames while pouring a libation of honey into the pit.

Come dawn, the unguent should be thinned with water and applied liberally all over the body. For a period of twenty-four hours thereafter the wearer was immune from all harms, be those harms intended by ferocious sword-wearing warriors or rabid flame-breathing bulls. Furthermore, the magical paste would grant superhuman strength and endurance for the same period.

Once she had delivered these instructions, as an apparent afterthought, Medea added that should Jason ever forget her after what she had done for him she would come to Jason's home in Iolcus and cast her reproaches personally into his face. Jason gamely took up the implied suggestion and gallantly suggested that were Medea ever to come to Iolcus, she would come as his bride. So far neither of the lovers had talked directly of Medea leaving Colchis but after this 'hypothetical' discussion the possibility was definitely on the table.

Preparations for the coming day intensified overnight, starting with the ritual performed by Jason. As the digging of a pit and the burning of the entire victim had doubtless informed our hero, Medea had instructed him to make his sacrifice to the cthonous gods, the Gods of the Underworld.

Medea may have failed to mention that in this case the sacrifice would get the personal attention of Medea's own patron and mentor, the witch-goddess Hecate.

And the dread goddess heard him from the profoundest deeps of the Underworld. In person she attended the sacrifice as Jason performed it. Countless torches seemed to flame around her and terrible serpents coiled themselves over her, and also over the branches of the oaks nearby. The ground trembled under her feet and the shrieks of the frightened nymphs of the river, marsh and meadow accompanied the baying of her infernal hounds. The terrified Jason did not turn to flee, but nevertheless his feet carried him backwards, and in this manner he returned to his companions just as the first light of dawn lit up the snowy peaks of the Caucasus mountains.

Argonautica 3.220

Meanwhile Aeëtes was making his own preparations. Doubtless word of his daughter's betrayal had reached him. Knowing Medea as he did, it would have been clear to Aeëtes that the coming challenge would no

SECURING THE FLEECE

longer be a walkover win for the oxen. Consequently Aeëtes prepared to fight for his Fleece. Even as the trembling Jason was rejoining his comrades Aeëtes was pulling on his leather-bound breastplate (a gift from Ares himself) and taking up his shield, sword and spear. Then, terrible in his warlike panoply, Aeëtes rode his chariot from the palace, secure in the knowledge that none on earth apart from mighty Hercules himself was capable of withstanding him. And of course, Hercules had gone home.

Aeëtes took up his station beside the river, on a bluff overlooking the Field of Ares where Jason had to yoke the bulls and sow the dragon's teeth. Right on time the *Argo* came arrowing up the river, propelled by a boatload of heroes inspired by the effect that the magical unguent was having upon their leader. Jason himself was at the prow, revelling in his newfound strength and tossing his shield and spear aloft, then out of sheer *joie de vivre* leaping up to retrieve them from the air.

And so to the challenge. Jason carefully stuck the sharpened butt-end of his spear into the ground and hung his helmet and sword upon it. Then with his shield alone he advanced upon the bulls. Were he not protected by Medea's magic, Jason's legend would have ended right then in a fiery barbecue upon the Field of Ares. As it was, the wondering Argonauts saw their leader vanish into a cloak of flame and smoke that resembled nothing so much as the opened door of a metal-smelting furnace. When the smoke cleared it was discovered that Jason had overcome both of Aeëtes' bovine flamethrowers and yoked them to the plough. Now he was using his spear as a goad to move the reluctant beasts into position for the first furrow.

Beneath the gaze of the furious Aeëtes Jason went about his business, driving the complaining oxen and putting his shoulder to the plough. All the while he kept dropping the dragon's teeth into the furrows and anxiously glancing over his shoulder in case the promised armed men should spring up before he had finished ploughing.

In fact it took the seeds the rest of the morning to germinate, allowing Jason time to pop back to the *Argo* for a quick lunch while the field became steadily populated with armed men rising from the earth. That part of the unguent which protected the wearer from harm had indeed worked like the charm it was. Now it remained to be seen whether Medea had done an equally good job with the superhuman speed and strength bit.

First Jason took Medea's advice on levelling the odds somewhat. He (or by some rival accounts Medea herself) lobbed a rock into the crowd of warriors from a place of concealment. Those hit by the rock were unable to tell from whence it had come and started blaming each other. Recriminations turned to blows, and soon the entire field had become a huge melee, with bodies dropping as fast as they sprang from the ground.

Into the chaos charged Jason like a human threshing machine, cutting down warriors right, left and centre. In such circumstances the only advantage a single fighter usually has against a group is that members of the group have to be careful not to hurt one another in the confusion. In this case, the warriors did not care who else got hurt and Jason could not be hurt anyway.

SECURING THE FLEECE

Therefore the efforts of the warrior band served only to further thin their rapidly-diminishing number. Towards the end of the fight Jason was cutting down warriors faster than they emerged from the earth, leaving the later corpses like gory, drooping statues unable to fall over completely as their legs were still embedded in the soil.

And so, remarks the poet, 'the day died, and Jason's challenge was ended.' The more interesting aftermath was about to begin.

Chapter 4

The Flight from Colchis

Jason had executed to perfection the task set for him by Aeëtes. Yet in that very perfection lay a problem. There was simply no way that Jason could have survived the task, let alone completed it to the letter, without magical help – and there was little doubt from whence that help had come. Watching Jason at work Aeëtes must have realized that the rumours were true and that his own daughter, Medea, had betrayed him.

Medea was formidable, but a furious Aeëtes was more formidable still. Rather than face her father's wrath Medea decided that it was time to take up Jason's suggestion that she join him on the return to his homeland. This was a prospect that Medea faced with ambivalence. On the one hand, she would be sailing off to adventure in a new world with her lover by her side. On the other hand she would be leaving behind her mother, her family and the only home she had ever known, and doing so under circumstances that made any return highly improbable.

So that night for the last time, Medea returned to her rooms. Her sorcerous talents allowed her to do that much unseen and there was a pharmacopoeia of potions that she had no wish to abandon. Before she departed, Medea left behind on her bed a long tress of her hair. This she expected her mother to find and the message was clear. It was the tradition of Greek girls

THE FLIGHT FROM COLCHIS

to cut a tress of their hair before marriage and dedicate that to the goddess Artemis.

From there Medea made her way out to her second home, the temple of Hecate. That the gates of the palace were barred was not a problem, for the bolts slid open and the doors, untouched, leapt backwards at the absent-minded application of Medea's magic. Still invisible to human eyes she hurried through the back streets of the city, leaving its towers and her old life behind.

Finally, having equipped herself at the temple with everything that a young magic-wielder needs before eloping, Medea made her way to the encampment by the river where the Argonauts were celebrating the improbable survival of their leader. The arrival of Medea, anguished and desolate though she was, delighted Jason.

Gently he took her up and embraced her while murmuring soft words of comfort. 'I swear to you, before Zeus of Olympus that you shall be my Lady. Let the God's consort Hera, goddess of marriage, witness that when we have returned to Hellas you will enter my home as a new-wed bride.'

Argonautica 4.92

Having obtained Jason's promise of marriage, Medea immediately became practical once more. Briskly she informed her fiancé that he would be waiting forever if he expected her father to hand over the Fleece as agreed. The only way that the Argonauts would obtain their prize was for them to take it – immediately, before Aeëtes realized that Jason was not going to make a formal claim.

Accordingly, before even the first light of dawn brightened the eastern sky, the *Argo* was propelled swiftly and silently upriver to the park where the Fleece was stored in its sacred grove. At the very place where the golden ram had deposited Phrixus after his flight from Greece, two people disembarked – Medea and a somewhat anxious Jason. Jason had good reason to be fearful, for the giant serpent which guarded the Fleece was every bit as dreadful as advertised.

There is some disagreement about what happened next. The most convincing tradition tells that Jason felt that he should be protective of his bride-to-be. Perhaps reasoning that the effects of his magical potion were not due to wear off for yet another hour or two, Jason immediately leapt forward to do battle with the monster. Though Jason was invulnerable, he quickly discovered that the serpent did not need to tear Jason apart to defeat him – it simply swallowed him whole. Then the beast settled down to wait for the potion to wear off and the process of digestion to begin.

Consuming a large meal often leads to sleepiness and in this case the serpent had literally eaten a heroic breakfast. Its drowsiness was further increased by the wiles of Medea who sang the serpent to sleep with a gently hypnotic lullaby. Weaving into her song prayers to Hecate, the night-wanderer, and Persephone, Queen of the Underworld, Medea quietly broke a branch from a nearby juniper bush. With her own powers she drew from the leaves their magical properties as she brushed the branch down the rapidly relaxing serpent's spine, along the ridges of its brow and over its man-eating jaws.

THE FLIGHT FROM COLCHIS

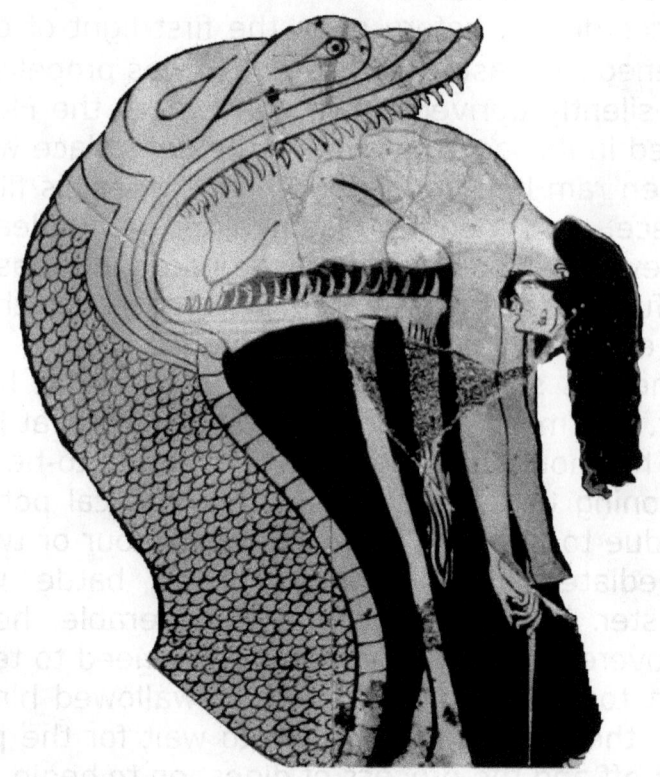

Breakfast of champions. Jason gets swallowed whole in this painting on a fifth-century Greek vase.

One of the reasons Medea had visited her temple one last time before she joined the Argonauts was to prepare for this very moment. Knowing that a confrontation with the serpent was inevitable, she had a potion ready for when she could convert a deep sleep into a drugged slumber. It was also fortunate that, among its other non-magical properties, *Juniperus Sabina Cupressacae* is also a powerful emetic. In his *Argonautica* the poet Apollonius Rhodius does not mention the swallowing of Jason, but nevertheless he does mention the juniper by which means Jason, if he was indeed swallowed, was caused to be vomited up once more into the land of the living.

From there, it was a simple matter for the somewhat stunned Jason to clamber up the coils of the comatose serpent, unhook the Golden Fleece from the oak bough upon which it hung, and run for it. Or rather stagger for it, since the Fleece was both large and extremely heavy and for the moment Medea could not help as she had to remain behind as a watchful anaesthetist to the Fleece's serpentine ex-guardian.

It would appear that when Medea finally departed, she left the serpent alive but in a coma. Nevertheless many modern accounts of the legend appear to think that Jason killed the serpent because that was the sort of thing that Greek heroes did. However, according to ancient accounts Jason was instead preoccupied with getting himself and his precious cargo back to the *Argo* at record speed. The situation was far too urgent for him to take the extra time for a completely unnecessary ophidicide. Indeed, the moment that Jason and Medea got back to the *Argo* (Medea had caught up with the burdened Jason easily enough), Jason quickly stilled any celebrations, ordered the crew to stop marvelling over the Fleece and get straight to the oars.

Sure enough, at that very moment the Colchians had become aware that they had been robbed of the Fleece and were flocking to the palace to demand that Aeëtes immediately retrieve their national treasure. Aeëtes was already on it, fully armoured and sending troops post-haste downriver to block the passage to the sea of the impudent Argonauts and his runaway daughter. Troops despatched, Aeëtes himself, terrible in his wrath, climbed upon his chariot and sent his horses flying like the wind down the road that ran alongside the river.

The *Argo* was the swiftest ship the world had yet ever seen and it was being propelled downriver by a muscular crew of highly-motivated heroes. Yet the river itself was unhelpful, with abundant dangerously shallow stretches which needed to be navigated with caution. Furthermore while the road was relatively direct the river covered almost twice the distance, curving from left to right as it wiggled towards the sea like a demented snake.

At this point in the tale of Apollonius Rhodius it is clear that someone had done their homework, for his description of the river Phasis is accurate - similar conditions exist today on that river (now the River Rioni in modern Georgia). Also, where the River Rioni now meets the Black Sea, the river breaks into a delta and the same was evidently true some three thousand years ago when the river was called the Phasis.

On the banks of the Phasis a detachment of Colchian archers had raced ahead of the fleeing *Argo*, and were lined up along the riverside ready to perforate the ship with a storm of arrows as it passed by. Naturally enough, the archers had expected that the *Argo* would take the direct route to the sea. This was by way of the river's northern channel where the water is deepest and the current swiftest, and the archers had set up their ambush accordingly.

Yet the crew had been warned by prophesy months ago that they would face their moment of greatest peril just as their ship left the river for the sea. The crew were already wary. Indeed, expecting just such an attack, Jason had ordered half the crew to keep rowing while half lined the ship's bulwarks in an attempt to guard the rowers with their shields. Yet so close must the *Argo* pass to the shore and so numerous were the archers that even Jason's precautions would not be enough.

Therefore Hera – who had been watching developments in Colchis with great interest – intervened to save her protege. The sun behind the Argonauts abruptly ceased to reflect off the waters of the northern channel, while the light on the slower, turgid southern channel doubled in intensity. The crew were quick to take the hint and sent the *Argo* flying safely down the divinely-marked southern detour. (Geographical information courtesy of *The Argonautica*, Apollonius Rhodius, Library of Alexandria, c.250 BC and the *Journal of Polish Agricultural Universities*, vol.5, issue 2, 2002 "Environmental Conditions Of Common Sturgeon (*Acipenser Sturio L.*) Spawning In River Rioni" by Ryszard Kolman and Zurab Zarkua)

Once the Argonauts had reached the open sea their peril was far from over. Aeëtes set about organizing a fleet of ships to set off in pursuit and delegated teams of rowers to work in shifts. The *Argo* might be powered by heroes, but even heroes have to rest and sleep while the crews of Aeëtes could do both, with some sleeping while others took over rowing duties. Yet even with these disadvantages the *Argo* managed to keep its nose ahead of the chasing pack and the pursuit went on for day after day with the ships traversing the northern shore of the Euxine (Black Sea) at record speed.

It is at this point that cruder modern versions of the legend of Medea inform us that the lady slowed down the ships of her father by hewing to pieces the body of her younger brother and dropping them over the side of the *Argo* so that her father was forced to slow down to retrieve the bits for a decent burial. This version of the legend should be immediately rejected. Firstly the sudden appearance of her younger brother begs the question of where Medea had stashed the lad up to this point. Secondly, there is the issue of how the whole 'dropping bits over the side' business would actually work.

Man overboard (in installments). Nineteenth-century painter Herbert Draper depicts the death of Absyrtus as it could not have happened.

Unless human physiology has changed dramatically in the last three thousand years, any forensic investigator will confirm that body parts tossed into water promptly sink to the bottom. In the case of the Euxine, without some sort of fiddly flotation device attached to each part, those brotherly bits would have vanished beneath the waves before Aeëtes was even aware of what was happening, let alone before he could retrieve them.

Furthermore those up to speed with Colchian mythology might raise another objection. The younger brother of Medea was no helpless pre-teen. He was Absyrtus, nicknamed 'Phaeton' by his peers because he outshone them all in his warlike strength and ability.

In the Colchian civil war which Aeëtes was waging with his brother Perses, the Scythians were at one point persuaded to weigh in on the side of Perses. It was young Absyrtus, clad in golden armour who drove his chariot into the midst of the Scythian host, breaking their formation and allowing the Colchian army to sweep the invaders from the battlefield. This sturdy young warrior was hardly a helpless child whom Medea could smuggle out of the palace under her cloak and park, uncomplaining, somewhere aboard the *Argo*.

In fact, far from being a helpless abductee, Absyrtus was leading the chase to retrieve Medea and the Fleece, though Aeëtes and the rest of the Colchian navy were not far behind.

At present Absyrtus had left the main body of the pack and cut ahead to where he was sure that the *Argo* was headed. This was the land of a people called the Minyans, a Helladic tribe once widespread across Greece, but now concentrated in only a few places. One of these was the lands on the western shore of the

THE FLIGHT FROM COLCHIS

Euxine just south of the mouth of the Danube (on the coast of modern Romania). The Minyans were allies of Colchis, and had given aid to Aeëtes in his recent wars. Yet despite the close relations between the two nations, the Minyans were not particularly happy to see Absyrtus. This was because the *Argo* had also recently made landfall and Jason and his heroes were currently guests of the Minyan king.

This put the King in an unhappy predicament. First of all the Colchians and Argonauts were quite prepared to fight it out right there and then – the only question was alongside whom, if anyone, the Minyans would fight. On the one hand, if the Minyans stayed neutral it was quite likely that Jason's band of battle-hardened heroes would make short work of Absyrtus and his advance party. This would lead to a number of pointed questions from the formidable Aeëtes when he arrived with the main fleet. Questions such as why his supposed ally had allowed his son to be killed, and why, through inaction the Minyans had abetted the actions of a gang of abductors and thieves?

On the other hand, if the Minyans sided with the Colchians, then it was Jason's heroes who would be cut down - and they would not go quietly. The Minyan army could expect to get quite severely dented in the process - and that issue would be just the start of their troubles. Among the heroes on the *Argo* were two sons of the king of Sparta, Athenian noblemen, Theban aristocrats and the scions of some of the leading houses of Greece. All of these noblemen would take a dim view of the king who had been instrumental in their sons' demise and might well club together to do something about it. In short the Minyans were damned if they did, and damned if they didn't. And that was before they contemplated the task of keeping an enraged and terrified Medea captive until her father could get his hands on her.

One version of what happened next is given in *Fabula* 23 of the *Fabulae* of the writer Hyginus.

Absyrtus caught up with Medea in the Adriatic Sea near Histria. She was at the court of King Alcinous when Absyrtus arrived and announced his intention of taking Medea by force. To prevent a pitched battle Alcinous offered to act as mediator and announced that he would give his decision on the morrow. That night the King's wife asked what her deeply depressed husband had decided. Alcinous informed her that in the end he had resolved that if the union of Jason and Medea had not been consummated, he would send Medea back to her father. If Medea was no longer a virgin, then he would consider this a de facto marriage, and order that Medea remain with Jason.

The wife promptly sent word to Jason of this decision and the pair immediately lay together that night in a cave. When the couple came to the King's court the next morning, Medea was found to be a wife and it was ordered that she remain with her husband. Absyrtus, fearing his father's wrath, continued the pursuit... .

Other writers such as the Roman poet Ovid have another take upon the matter, as does our main source for these events, Apollonius Rhodius. A synthesis of these different stories gives us an equally probable account of what happened next and this is given below.

THE FLIGHT FROM COLCHIS

When Absyrtus arrived in the land of the Minyans he - as already described – announced his intention of completing his mission by force if need be. To bring the Minyans onto his side he implied that his father's main objective was to retrieve his runaway daughter and thereafter possession of the Golden Fleece was negotiable. This appeal to the king's cupidity tipped the scales and he declared the Minyans to be on the Colchian side.

Jason and his heroes prepared to fight to the death, but Jason being Jason, decided to try diplomacy first, Accordingly he presented an alternative proposal to the king. What if the Argonauts handed over Medea to her brother and then slipped away with the Fleece before the arrival of Aeëtes? Absyrtus had already declared that recapturing Medea was his main purpose and the partial completion of the mission would calm Aeëtes to the point where he might simply continue his pursuit of the *Argo* without troubling the Minyans any further.

By this proposal everyone would get something of what they wanted, while – as with all the best negotiated settlements - leaving everyone a bit dissatisfied. Except, that is, for Medea, who was not at all dissatisfied. She was livid and let Jason know it in no uncertain terms. Gently Jason tried to pacify his outraged partner.

He acknowledged that Medea had been instrumental in getting him the Fleece and had saved his life twice before that - once with the oxen and once with the serpent. Now it was time for Medea to save him yet again. The only choices on offer were that Medea be handed over as a prisoner to her brother while Jason and his crew escaped unharmed with the Fleece, or alternatively, that Medea be taken prisoner by her brother while Jason and his crew lay dead on the battlefield. As a loving wife, which option did she prefer?

Medea's answer takes up several dozen lines of poetry, but can be summarized as follows. Firstly Jason should clearly understand that he was an ungrateful, cowardly swine. Regrettably, he was the ungrateful, cowardly swine that Medea was stuck with. Therefore Jason should stick to doing what had worked well for him up to now – namely, he should shut up, leave the heavy thinking to Medea and do exactly as he was told.

Shortly thereafter Absyrtus received a clandestine message from Medea suggesting that perhaps she could work with him to restore the Golden Fleece to Aeëtes. In exchange she wanted him to accept her claim that the Argonauts and the children of Phrixus had kidnapped her from Colchis and she had been their unwilling prisoner ever since. Then shortly afterwards Jason presented himself in person to Absyrtus as a Greek bearing gifts, with the gift in question being a magnificent cloak that Jason informed Absyrtus was a peace-offering from his sister.

At this meeting of unbrotherly brothers-in-law, Jason remarked that the entire chase was wearing the Argonauts down. As to Medea, it seemed she no longer wanted anything to do with Argonauts or Colchians. She had taken herself to a small island just off the coast and was there at the temple of Artemis, the maiden goddess, praying somehow to be rescued from her desperate dilemma. That is, Jason stressed – and

THE FLIGHT FROM COLCHIS

one can imagine him giving Absyrtus a long, significant look at this point – Medea was there on the island, alone.

It would not have been hard for Absyrtus to join the dots. Evidently the tempestuous passion of Jason and Medea had cooled dramatically once the pair were stuck in one another's company day after day on the *Argo*. Medea wanted to get shot of Jason just as much as Jason wanted to be rid of Medea. So now she had conveniently withdrawn to an isolated island and was there for the taking. Hopefully she could be captured by false promises and soft words, for the idea of keeping an enraged Medea prisoner until her father arrived was not a pleasant prospect. Then, with Medea handed over to Aeëtes for punishment, Absyrtus could resume his pursuit of Jason and his impudent Argonauts, retrieve the Fleece and return to Colchis in triumph.

So that night a shipload of Colchian troops quietly grounded their vessel on the beach of the sacred Isle of Artemis. Leaving his crew on the shore, Absyrtus proceeded alone to the temple, perhaps reasoning that Medea would be less intimidated if just Absyrtus came to take her home without the threat of armed retainers. Also, of course, Medea's messages had dropped tantalizing hints that she might be induced to betray Jason and deliver the Fleece into his hands. This was a possibility Absyrtus wanted to explore further without witnesses to his planned treachery.

The young warrior came across Medea sitting quietly beside some bushes outside the temple of the Goddess. She seemed subdued, but not displeased to see her brother once more. Like a man dipping a foot into a fast-flowing stream, Absyrtus carefully began to check whether it was safe to go further without being swept away by the raging torrent of his sister's magic. Gently he coaxed her into agreeing to come home. Then, when she appeared amenable to the idea, Absyrtus carefully sounded out Medea on the possibility of somehow tricking Jason so that her 'abductor' and the Fleece ended up in his power.

The two talked quietly while Medea ascertained that Absyrtus saw nothing morally wrong with the treacherous betrayal of someone she had once loved. Once this point had been clearly established, Medea gave a pre-arranged signal and Jason stepped silently from the bushes, naked sword in hand. As pitilessly as a butcher kills his sacrificial animal victim outside a temple, Jason cut down the surprised Absyrtus, whose only warning had come when Medea abruptly turned away, covering her face so that she might not see her brother's bloody demise. This was the only part of her plan which failed, for as he fell to his knees the dying Absyrtus cupped his lifeblood in his palms and splashed it against Medea's face, turning her silvery veil to dripping crimson gore.

And the heroic son of Aeson cut from the corpse the hands and feet. Three times he licked up the dead man's blood and three times spat it from his teeth, as the slayer should do when he wishes to remove the pollution of a treacherous murder.

Argonautica 4.475

There was further butchering yet to be done, so Medea left Jason to his grisly task and walked to a headland overlooking the beach. Once there she lifted high a flaming torch. This was the prearranged signal for the *Argo* to come swiftly out of the shadows and run aground on the beach, stopping alongside the ship of Absyrtus. Like kites descending upon a flock of wood-pigeons the heroes swooped upon the confused Colchians, most of whom were dead before they even realized that they were fighting for their lives. Not one of the Colchian crew remained alive when Jason and Medea returned once more to the beach, having completed further gory arrangements for their escape.

Once word reached the mainland that Absyrtus was dead, the remainder of his advance party made an effort to resume the chase. However, the men were leaderless and doubtless somewhat demoralized. A convenient thunderstorm on the horizon gave them a pretext to abandon their pursuit, since the men could claim to have been held back by the 'lightnings of Hera'. Realizing that Aeëtes might find this excuse somewhat lame, the men of the Colchian advance party decided that rather than face their king they would find new homes elsewhere. 'Some settled on the islands and there their descendants live still, calling themselves the people of Absyrtus after their fallen leader. Others built an enclosed city by the deep river of shadowy Illyria, near the tomb of Harmonia and Cadmus', the poet informs us.

To Aeëtes, when he arrived with his fleet soon afterwards, it seemed as though his son and the advance party had vanished into thin air. Diligent enquiries established that Absyrtus had last been seen *en route* to the Isle of Artemis, so thence Aeëtes took himself and his fleet. Approaching the beach the Colchian king was confronted by a gruesome sight.

He [Absyrtus] *had been torn apart,*
Scattered were his limbs across the fields
And in many places besides.
[so] *That his father might realize this,*
High on a rock she [Medea] *had set his bloodless hands*
And bloodstained head.

Ovid, Tristia 3.9

The message was clear – if Aeëtes wanted to give his son a decent burial he would have to scour the island in a sort of ghastly treasure hunt until all the scattered body parts could be reassembled. Then the remains of his son could be burned on a pyre and the ashes properly deposited in a tomb. Only thereafter would Aeëtes be free to resume his hunt for the Argonauts, By then Jason was long gone and the trail was cold.

Despite this, the vengeful Aeëtes was to take his quest to the other side of Greece, by some accounts getting as far as the land of the Phoceans – modern Corfu - in the Adriatic. There the hunt ended, for news came from Colchis that, with the king and much of the army absent from the land, resistance to the usurper Perses had collapsed. Perses was now King of Colchis and Aeëtes had now become a dispossessed exile. Ironically, this had largely come about because Aeëtes had killed Phrixus in response to the prophecy that a family member would betray him - when as it turned out, Phrixus was the just about only person in the family of Aeëtes who did not do so in some way.

A further historical note is that the poet Ovid claims

that the killing of Absyrtus happened where the city Ovid was living in was later founded. He says that this city was called Tomis, from the Greek meaning 'sliced', a reference to the fate of Absyrtus. Tomis is now the city of Constanta, one of the largest ports in modern Romania.

Chapter 5

The Long Journey to Greece

Their flight from Aeëtes had taken the Argonauts far off course, so once the peril had lifted the crew began the measured process of making their way back home to Greece. Island after island vanished into the horizon behind their wake, Issa, Dysceladus and lovely Pityeia, then Melite of the soft zephyrs and rocky Cerossus. Then, as the island of Nymphea appeared in the distance, things went terribly wrong.

Mighty Zeus had become aware of events in the Euxine and had immediately recognized that the schemes of his wife lay behind them. Close questioning of Hera revealed the entire sordid story, including the circumstances leading to the betrayal and death of Medea's brother, Absyrtus. Zeus was outraged and prepared a mighty storm with which to sink the *Argo* and send the fratricidal Medea to a watery grave.

That the rest of the Argonauts also would go down with the ship did not trouble Zeus greatly. He, like most Greek gods, never let collateral damage - however extensive - get in the way of a good smiting. However, the prospect certainly alarmed Hera who was well aware that her favourite, Jason, would be aboard when the *Argo* went down with all hands. Therefore she pre-empted Zeus with a storm of her own which caught up the *Argo* like a toy in a bathtub and tossed boat and crew onto a rocky beach on the Isle of Electra, shaken but unharmed.

When the stunned Argonauts asked themselves what they had done to deserve such misfortune, the *Argo* itself answered by means of the oaken keel which had been taken from the sacred grove of Dodona, site of the oracle of Zeus himself. Granted human speech by Athena, the ship informed the Argonauts that their transgression had been to abet the murder of Absyrtus. The only reason that they were not right now breathing seawater was due to some hasty negotiations between Hera and her husband. Basically the Argonauts could expect nothing but ferocious storms and headwinds that would forever prevent their return to Greece unless they temporarily abandoned the effort to get home and instead sought out the Isle of Aeaea – home of the enchantress Circe.

As previously described, Circe was a formidable demi-goddess with a penchant for turning uninvited arrivals to her island into swine. In later years she became best known to posterity as the lover of wandering Odysseus. Through her sister Pasiphae of Crete, Circe was to become aunt to the dreaded Minotaur, but for the moment it was more significant that Circe was also the sister of Aeëtes. This made her also the aunt of the late Absyrtus and, as a family member of the deceased and a powerful magic user in her own rite, Circe was Medea's only chance of purifying herself and the Argonauts from the blood-guilt of fratricide.

News of their potential reprieve did not come as a great relief to the Argonauts, mainly because the isle of Circe lay far away, somewhere in the mists of distant Ausonia (as contemporary Greeks called the lands of the barbarian west). It would be a perilous journey just to get there, while Circe was rightly reputed to be more than somewhat perilous herself.

In fact, once the poesy is stripped out of the saga of the *Argo's* trip westwards it becomes clear that the journey traversed the entire Mediterranean. Indeed at one point Hera had to hastily leap down from the heavens, perch atop the Rock of Gibraltar, and yell at the Argonauts that they were taking a wrong turn into the Atlantic Ocean. Realizing that she needed to take a direct hand in navigating the *Argo* thereafter, Hera guided the ship back past the land of the Celts and Ligurians and, after a particularly strenuous rowing session, allowed the crew to rest at the island of Aethelia (modern Elba).

The heroes sat on the shore while the sweat dripped off them and under the magical influence of the island this sweat turned to pebbles as it landed on the beach. This is the explanation given in ancient times of why this beach of Aethelia was covered with pale white pebbles. Even today anyone who wishes to walk upon the petrified sweat of Jason's heroes need only take a stroll along Elba's delightful beach of Le Ghiale before enjoying a dip in water as crystal clear as it was when the *Argo* is said to have beached there millennia before.

As the Argonauts approached their destination, her magical powers informed Circe that something terrible was approaching her secluded island. As the bow wave precedes a ship, Medea's magic, polluted with the taint of murder, disturbed the sleep of Circe even before her

Circe depicted in the Neo-romantic style beloved of artists of the Victorian era.

niece made landfall. Circe dreamed that flames were sweeping across her collection of magical herbs and potions and that the walls of her home were running with blood. To defend her magical pharmacopoeia Circe drew upon her own blood and sprayed this across the flames. Then, because with magic users such as she, the line between reality and dream became somewhat blurred, Circe awoke needing to wash her blood-splattered hair and night-clothes.

Thus the Argonauts first beheld Circe at the sea's edge, washing her hair in the spray of the waves that broke on the rocks before her. Uneasy as she was, Circe had guarded herself with creatures which she had conjured from the slime on the beach, strange entities, half-formed and unlike any natural animal. They thronged about her like sheep around a shepherd in a shapeless jumble of limbs. The awed Argonauts who beheld this sight from their ship found little difficulty in believing that this was indeed the sister of mighty Aeëtes.

Circe had only to set eyes on Medea to know the power which had disturbed her sleep. Without speaking she turned back to her home, indicating with a gesture that the others should follow. Jason quickly assessed the odds and decided that Circe heavily outnumbered his fifty or so heavily-armed heroes. Therefore he told the crew to wait on the beach, took Medea's hand and proceeded with her down the path as a supplicant who awaited his fate.

Circe was already seated in her hall when the pair crossed her threshold. With a gesture she directed them to sit in chairs arranged before her. Like schoolchildren awaiting punishment, the two scuttled to their places and sat. Medea hid her face in her hands while Jason, not daring to look up, unsheathed the sword with which he had killed Absyrtus, set the point on the ground before him and then sat with his head bowed over the hilt. Still Circe had not spoken a word.

The enchantress did not need to. She could see what mortals could not, that behind Jason and Medea were the shadows of the Furies, dread avengers from a primaeval era. Two generations of gods previously, the proto-god Uranus and been overthrown from his kingship of the cosmos by his son Cronus – the father of Zeus. Cronus had crept up on his sleeping father, castrated him with a sickle and then thrown the amputated parts from the heavens into the sea.

From the foam where they fell had arisen Aphrodite, the Goddess of Love – but also the dark Furies, three primordial forces dedicated to the destruction of those who perpetrated injustice, especially injustice upon another family member. Jason's polluted sword and the attentive Furies told Circe all that she needed to know.

Cronus had replaced his crippled father as lord of the universe, yet even Cronus had been unable to keep the Furies from enacting their vengeance, which is why Cronus was overthrown in his turn by Zeus. So it was no small matter for Circe to get the Furies off the case of the supplicants before her, and do this whilst simultaneously assuaging the anger of Zeus. Fortunately for Medea, her world was a rough place which had afforded plentiful opportunities for trial and error in rituals involving blood-guilt, and Circe being Circe, the enchantress was up to speed with the state of the art.

Several complicated sacrifices and rites later, Circe was reasonably sure that the vengeance of Zeus was off the table. After all Zeus himself had a few killings of which he was not proud and had on occasion incited others to perform similarly dark deeds. Furthermore, Zeus was the God of Supplicants, and when two supplicants came with propitiation offered by Circe, daughter of Helios the Sun God, it was easy for Zeus to stay his wrath. The Furies were another matter. They were a primordial force of nature, impervious to reason, flattery or threat. Circe did what she could, but as it turned out even the best efforts of the most powerful of enchantresses merely moved Jason and Medea from the 'immediate action' file to 'cases pending'. Doom was not averted, but merely deferred.

Immediate business concluded, Circe took the opportunity to settle down for a long chat with her niece. Mostly this chat took the form of Circe listening quietly while Medea poured out the story of Jason's adventures with the Argonauts before they came to Colchis, the struggle for the Fleece, and the desperate race to escape the fury of Aeëtes. The deed that had brought Medea to Circe, the murder of her brother, was lightly glossed over. That part Circe had been able to figure out for herself.

When all had been said and done, Circe sat quietly for a while. Then with a deep sigh she addressed her sobbing niece. There was much to sympathize with in Medea's actions – she had not acted for personal gain but out of love for Jason and the children of Phrixus. Aeëtes was a brute and once Medea had stolen his Fleece any sane person would have taken to their heels and fled as Medea had done. Nevertheless.

Whatever charitable interpretation Medea might give her actions, the underlying facts were inescapable. She had betrayed her father. She had turned traitor to her country when she not only allowed its national treasure to be taken but had been instrumental in that taking. From those actions, others had followed inexorably – in taking the Fleece Medea had taken from Aeëtes the symbol of kingship, and her father had duly lost his kingdom. In taking the Fleece Medea had known that pursuit was inevitable and capture quite probable and she had done the unthinkable rather than let that happen.

As mentioned already, the world of heroic Greece was a rough place - and it did not accept excuses. Hera had driven Hercules mad, and in his madness Hercules had slain his own children. No matter that this was the last thing that Hercules had wanted or that he was helpless to prevent it - he had done it and he was responsible. The famous Labours were performed in expiation. In later years Oedipus would blind himself as a self-inflicted punishment for killing his father and sleeping with his mother, even though all concerned had tried mightily to prevent exactly that from happening. So, for Medea the fact that she could do nothing other than as she had done once Cupid's arrow had pierced her breast was no excuse. She had done what she had done, and she was guilty.

Softly Circe explained, 'Medea, no matter what your motives, your deeds are shameful and evil. Intolerable though they are, you are here as a supplicant and a kinswoman and certainly you need fear no harm from me. But I can't approve your actions or your abandonment of home and country. You have chosen to go with this stranger, so now you must go with him. You are no longer welcome here. Begone.'

Gently though it was delivered, nothing could disguise the harshness of Circe's judgement. Jason and Medea were subdued as they left the abode of the enchantress, but Hera, who had been closely following events, was delighted. That the wrath of the Furies had been merely postponed was of little concern to the goddess, for she needed Medea and Jason in play for only so long as it took for her to realize the end for which she had put the whole business in motion – the overthrow of the impious king of Iolcus. What happened to Medea thereafter was not something that greatly concerned Hera.

For now though, Hera's energies were focussed on getting the *Argo* and the Golden Fleece back to Thessaly as soon as possible. There were a number of perils in the seas between the heroes and their destination and Hera was determined to make sure that they circumnavigated them all. Therefore her first order of business lay with the watery court of Poseidon. While Hera was not on particularly good terms with her brother (she had once inveigled him into a plot to overthrow Zeus, and proud Poseidon was still smarting from Zeus' punishment), Hera did have an ally in Poseidon's retinue.

This was Thetis the sea nymph, a demi-goddess who pops up in a number of myths. In one case Hera, disgusted with the deformity of her new-born son Hephaestus the future craftsman god, tossed the infant from Olympus. (In very many ways, Hera was not a nice person.) It was Thetis who retrieved the crippled god from the waves into which he fell and reared him as a surrogate mother. Even Zeus had considered seducing Thetis (that is, raping her – he never took 'no' for an answer). He hastily backed away from the idea when Prometheus had revealed that any son of Thetis would be mightier than his father. Zeus, like any ancient autocrat, was none too secure on his throne. Since he had gained that throne by overthrowing his father, just as his father had overthrown his grandfather, Zeus found the prospect of fathering a son mightier than himself distinctly unappealing.

Thetis herself was none too thrilled about the prospect of sex with Zeus and therefore was rather concerned with the well-being of one of the heroes on Jason's boat. This was Peleus, the hero whom she was destined to marry (incidentally starting the Trojan War in the process) and who would father the mighty warrior Achilles. None of this would happen if Peleus came to a sticky end on one of the many hazards lying in wait between the *Argo* and safe haven in Greece, and Thetis really did not want to become single and available once more.

Therefore, she and Hera worked together to persuade the Neriads to calm the waves and to give the *Argo* a following sea. The wind was persuaded to blow always from the west as Hera used her divine influence to ensure that the *Argo* and its precious cargo got home before anything else went wrong. Next, Peleus on the *Argo* was granted a quick visit from his beloved who informed him that, weather-wise, the fix was in and the heroes should start propelling their ship eastwards at high speed while the going was good.

The first danger appeared almost at once as the *Argo* cruised past the beautiful island of Antiphemoessa, the very name of which isle signalled the peril on its shores. 'Antiphemoessa' is derived from the Greek word *antiphona*, meaning a song with a call and response. (From whence comes the English word 'anthem'). In this case the call from Antiphemoessa was literally a siren song, for unlike their unmelodious modern descendants which perch upon police cars and ambulances, the song of the ancient Sirens was sweet and irresistibly seductive. Those who heard the Sirens singing would immediately forget all else in their desire to get closer, leap over the gunwales of their ships and drown in the reefs surrounding the island. Survivors simply sat in ecstasy on the beach listening to the music until they wasted away from hunger and thirst. Exactly what the Sirens got out this is uncertain.

As mentioned earlier, Odysseus was to arrive in these parts a generation later and forewarned by Circe, he ordered his crewmen to block the Sirens' song by temporarily deafening themselves with wax earplugs. The Argonauts were able to do even better because their crew included Orpheus. As the greatest musician who ever twanged a lyre. Orpheus was able to produce music at least a match for the Sirens' best efforts and he was closer, being seated on the boat itself. Unfortunately the hero Butes, sitting in the stern, was closer to the Sirens and before anyone realized that he had been affected he abruptly threw himself overboard and began swimming for the shore.

Luckily Aphrodite had also been keeping up with Medea's adventures ever since Hera had roped the love goddess into her schemes. Butes had a saltwater ancestry (his mother Zeuxippe was a Neriad) and he was himself a priest of Poseidon. Therefore it was easy enough for Aphrodite to persuade the sea to give up its victim, after which Aphrodite whipped him to safety in Sicily. Nevertheless, the Argonauts were short a crewman and chastened to realize that they had suffered this casualty from the least of the perils which awaited them.

Next came Mt Etna, and certain doom for any ship

that passed by. The first problem was that Hephaestus had his smithy beneath the mountain and consequently the sea around was blanketed with a dense smog of smoke from his fires. This presented a hazard to navigation, certainly, for no sailor likes to be on a lee coast with bad visibility ('lee', because it will be remembered that the wind was blowing from the west). However, Mt Etna also produced pumice in rocks of prodigious size and quantity, and these floated invisibly in the smog like icebergs of stone waiting to doom any unwary ship that wandered against or between them.

Finally, should good fortune carry a ship beyond these hazards there awaited rough seas on the other side, though 'rough' is a considerable understatement. So high did the waves get that their tops brushed the clouds while particularly deep troughs revealed the sea bottom below. For all this Hera had prepared. The Argonauts could avoid a lengthy detour and cut right through these danger zones.

Hephaestus had been persuaded to stop work for the day, and was sat on the mountainside, hammer resting against his shoulder, to watch the *Argo* sail by. Meanwhile the Neriads yanked the ship this way and that as they steered the *Argo* through the hazard of the wandering rocks. Then, as the seas grew rougher and rougher, the Neriads changed tack. As maidens at a sandy beach played with a ball in the shallows by rolling their dresses up past their waists so that they could sport in the water, so the Neriads girded their loins and each took a wave. Just as the maidens would toss the ball from hand to hand, so the Neriads flicked the *Argo* from wave-crest to wave-crest, sending the ship skimming over the foam while the watching Hera wrapped her arms around Athena in excitement and dread until the *Argo* reached the safety of smoother waters.

Things went smoothly for a while after that, with Medea being hospitably received at Drepane (Corfu). As 'Drepna' the name of the island meant 'sickle' because its curved shape caused the inhabitants to believe that they dwelt upon the very sickle which Cronus had cast away once he had castrated Uranus. Here Medea and Jason formally celebrated their wedding in a splendid ceremony hosted by the island's king – much to the discomfiture of those Colchians from the pursuit squadron sent out by Aeëtes who had made it thus far. (These last survivors of the Great Chase now threw in the towel, abandoned their efforts and settled down to live among the locals.)

Those who wish to follow in the wake of the *Argo* can visit the cave where Medea and Jason spent the night before their wedding. The cave is now called Grava, and it lies to the west of Lake Korisson near the Byzantine fortress of Gardiki. Gone are the altars to Apollo which Medea set up in a local temple to commemorate the happy occasion, though sacrifices were reportedly performed at these throughout antiquity. The wedding was a blissfully happy respite from the unrelieved grim terror which had dogged Medea and the Argonauts from the moment they had fled from Colchis. Yet this pleasant sojourn came at a price, for while Medea and Jason partied on Corfu the time allotted for a gentle sea and favourable winds came to an end.

THE LONG JOURNEY TO GREECE

The Argo under sail in a painting by Konstantinos Volanakis (1837-1907)

It was still a beautiful day when the *Argo* put to sea once more, with the island's king and cheering crowds waving them farewell from the harbour. But as the coastline of Hellas finally came into sight the weather turned ugly. A gale came howling down from the eastern Alps and it pushed the *Argo* ever southward across the Mediterranean through nine days and nights of frantic rowing and bailing. Eventually the ship and its exhausted crew ended up becalmed in the waters of Syrtis (the modern Gulf of Sidra) off the coast of Libya, a place known to ancient mariners with the somewhat ominous subtitle of 'The Bay from Whence No Ships Return'.

To say that the ship was in the 'waters' of Syrtis was something of an exaggeration, for there was barely enough seawater to cover the keel - which was in any case dug deep into the sand below. The heroes and Medea climbed from the ship into knee-deep water and took stock of their situation. It was not good.

Almost on the horizon was the shore, separated from the *Argo* by mile after mile of sandbanks and shoals, over which ran little more than the foam from the seawater. Great masses of seaweed thrown up by the storm blocked the few passages in the maze. And should the Argonauts eventually struggle to the beach they would find themselves in one of the most desolate shores in North Africa – a place where centuries later the Roman Cato the Younger would almost lose an army to thirst and snakebite.

Yet at the same time even the breeze blowing from land to sea was useless, for the *Argo* had been carried into the shoals by the unnaturally high waters of the storm which had taken them south. Now that the storm had abated, the ship was stuck high and dry far from the nearest navigable waters. Even another storm would not help their case, because the same wind that would raise the waters would be blowing too hard to the south for the *Argo* to struggle against it out of the trap. Being Greeks, the Argonauts were expert sailors almost to a man, and to a man they each took stock of their situation and agreed it was hopeless.

The Argonauts had been through a lot and their morale had plummeted to sea-bottom levels. To have been actually within sight of Greece when the storm struck had been the final blow that had broken their spirit. The men left Medea to herself on the deck and each wandered off to find a comfortable place on the dunes where they intended literally to curl up and die. As the chief of this gallant band Jason led by example, wrapping himself in his cloak and lying in solitary misery through the night.

Yet soon after dawn he was awakened by a breeze that lifted his cloak from his head. Then Jason imagined that he heard the voice of the guardian spirits of the land telling him - once the poetry is stripped from their gentle chiding – to man up, trust in the Gods and figure out an escape from their predicament. Accordingly Jason called his heroes together for a conference and while various options were being discussed, the crew were astonished to see a white horse gallop through the foam towards the land. Turtles, dolphins and sea bass are the main denizens of the bay (which has an area of over 20,000 square miles). Horses are something of an exception so the Argonauts took keen note of the route and direction of the animal's travel, assuming that the beast must have been sent as a guide by Poseidon, God of horses and the sea.

Thereafter there was no option but to follow where the horse had led and since it was unthinkable that they should leave their ship behind, the heroes simply picked the *Argo* up and carried it with them. In historical times there are examples of even much heavier triremes being transported in this manner, so this is certainly not a mythical exaggeration. Assuming a good supply of water stored aboard and abundant marine life in the shallows, it is also not impossible to imagine that the crew managed the twelve-day journey to the shore.

What the crew were hoping was that the horse indicated that they were not far from Lake Tritonis. This was a large inshore lake off the Gulf that is mentioned by a number of writers in antiquity - not only by wild-eyed tellers of myth but also by serious geographers such as Ptolemy (*Geog.* 4.3.19) and Strabo (17.3.1). It is believed that the lake actually existed, but an earthquake after AD 600 broke the natural dike between the lake and the Mediterranean, draining the waters into the sea and leaving today's dry basin which goes by the name of *Schibkah-el-Lovdjah*.

Once they had reached the shore the heroes scattered, looking for a stream, a spring, or any other source of water. Instead they eventually came across a scene of desolation. Had the heroes arrived just a few days earlier they would have found a beautiful garden, a green oasis of music and beauty created by Gaia to mark the occasion of the wedding of Zeus and Hera. 'Where the God Oceanus denies further travel to the voyager, and giant Atlas holds the edge of the Earth, here the streams flow with ambrosia and Gaia gives to the gods blessed fruitfulness', says Euripides of this place in his play *Hippolytus* (l.745).

Now the streams had dried up and where the grove

had once resounded with singing the heroes heard only sobs. The sobbing came from three (or five, or seven, depending on the teller of the myth) nymphs who were the denizens of the grove. These were the Hesperides, minor Goddesses of the Evening to whom the first night of marriage was especially sacred. They were clustered about the base of a fallen apple tree, and the still-twitching corpse of a giant serpent.

It transpired that, as with many other scenes of devastation in the landscape of myth, what had happened was Hercules. For his eleventh labour he had been sent to collect apples from the garden of the Hesperides. He had accomplished this with the same subtlety as he had used to collect the horses of Diomedes (#Labour #8) the girdle of Hippolyta (Labour #9), and the cattle of Geryon (Labour #10) - which is to say he had arrived, killed whomever or whatever stood between him and his objective, taken his booty and departed. The now-deceased serpent had been a pet of the Hesperides and had the misfortune of also being the guardian of the apple tree which held the golden apples that Hercules needed to complete his quest.

The Argonauts rushed toward the scene of the crime but at their approach the grief-stricken Hesperides vanished in clouds of dust. It took a while, but eventually Orpheus was able to coax the nymphs back with soothing tunes on his lyre. The Argonauts asked what had happened to the Garden but also asked - with a great deal more urgency – what had happened to the water, and whether there was any further supply thereabouts. One of the nymphs explained.

'There came an evil, violent monster clad in a raw

lionskin, and with his bow he killed our serpent here. He had arrived on foot and was also looking for water, but could not find it anywhere. Eventually he came to one of the rocky cliffs holding back the Tritonian lake and stove in the base with a kick. Immediately the water came gushing out in full flow, and the monster laid himself on his chest and drank a mighty draught. After that ...'.

But by then the nymph was addressing the empty air, for the heroes had rushed off in the footsteps of Hercules to drink their fill at the newly-created spring. Then, refreshed and restocked with water, the crew continued with their arduous task of lugging their ship up to the lake. They did however spend some time looking around for Hercules since that mighty hero could carry their ship to the lake as easily as a hiker carries a backpack. However, only one of the scattered searchers caught a glimpse of him – a lonely figure already miles in the distance, trudging away through the trackless wasteland.

Thereafter the heroes struggled to the lake by themselves and re-launched the *Argo* upon its waters. They spent a while on Lake Tritonis searching for an outlet to the sea, which Triton himself revealed after a suitable sacrifice. At the outlet the heroes paused and built altars to Poseidon and Triton (altars which the poet assures us remained in his day as treasured relics in the little harbour town which later developed at the site). Then the Argonauts set their course for home, keeping the coast on their right and the south wind in their sails as they tacked north-eastwards across the Mediterranean towards the island of Crete.

Chapter 6

The Next Obstacle
Crete and Talos

The island of Crete was no mere way-station on the Argonauts' journey back to civilization. At this time, in the opinion of both the tellers of myth and modern archaeologists, Crete was a much more civilized place than Greece itself. According to the 5th century Greek historian Thucydides, the island was dominated by its major city of Knossos, a city which also had an established hegemony over nearby islands and parts of the eastern seaboard of mainland Greece - including Athens.

Modern historians are inclined to agree with the verdict of Thucydides, and pottery from Crete can be found right across the region, which suggests at the very least extensive trade and the wealth which usually accompanies it. Also, the remains of the Bronze Age palace at Knossos are indicative of a powerful and very wealthy state. The civilization in Crete at this time is usually referred to as Minoan, a reference to the mythological ruler of Crete, King Minos.

King Minos was a relative of Medea by marriage, for his wife was the lady Pasiphae, the sister of Aeëtes and Circe. As with her niece, Pasiphae possessed magical powers, though to a lesser extent than Medea and Circe. Pasiphae had her own problems, which were also related to infidelity. While she could honestly claim that she had slept with no man other than her husband, this claim loses much of its force once it is admitted that her extra-marital affair had been not with a man but a bull. An exceptionally handsome bull, and a paragon of its kind, but a bull nevertheless. (Pasiphae's misplaced lust was inflicted upon her because of a grudge held by Poseidon as the result of a complicated religious/political issue which need not concern us here.)

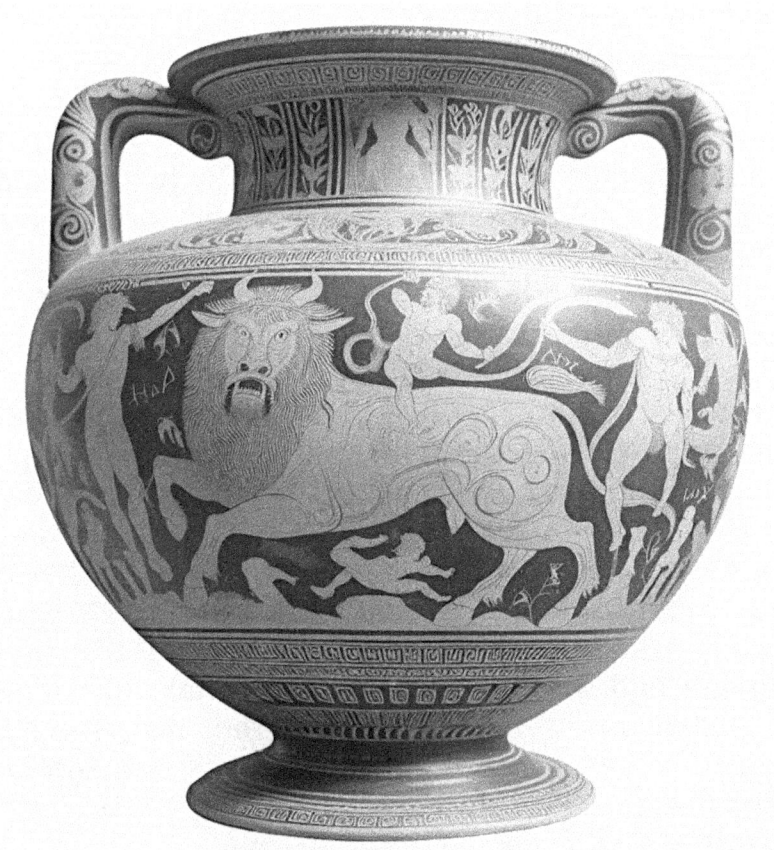

Pasiphae's lover, the Bull of Marathon shown on a hydria vase.

THE NEXT OBSTACLE – CRETE AND TALOS

This bull was eventually removed from the island by Hercules in the course of another of his labours. However its legacy lived on in the form of an embarrassing love-child from the strange coupling, a child called Asterios. Asterios was born with three major handicaps, each of which disqualified him from civilized company; a savage temper, a craving for human flesh, and the head of a bull set upon a powerful human body. This disfigurement gave the monstrous child the nickname by which he is known today – the Minotaur.

King Minos was persuaded by Pasiphae not to destroy his step-child but obviously this semi-human monstrosity could not be allowed to roam free. Accordingly the monster was kept in a twisting maze called the Labyrinth from which none who entered could ever find the exit.

Meanwhile another son of Pasiphae and Minos had headed for Athens, possibly out of a desire to escape the highly strained atmosphere at home. He competed at the local athletic festival in Athens and won almost every prize. So successful was this young man that he was murdered by his jealous competitors, a killing which brought an enraged King Minos and the Cretan fleet down upon the Athenians. The terrified Athenians tried to persuade Minos that his son had been killed when he had attempted to control the bull with which Pasiphae had mated. Hercules had simply turned that bull loose when he had completed his labour by bringing it to Greece, and the beast was now terrifying everyone on the plain of Marathon north-east of Athens.

King Minos did not believe this story and was

unimpressed with the Athenian attempt to deflect his wrath by bringing up his wife's unfortunate romantic history. To save their city the Athenians were forced to pay Midas a tribute – every five years a contingent of unfortunate young men and women were to be shipped to Crete. This would satisfy Minos' desire for revenge for the death of his son and simultaneously satisfy his step-son's cannibalistic lust.

Minos might have worried that this dreadful tribute and similar exactions from the peoples subject to the rule of Knossos might eventually produce a rebellion. However, Crete was safe from invasion thanks to the protection of Talos.

The Giant Talos armed with a stone. Silver didrachm from Phaistos, Crete (ca. 300/280-270 BC). Photographer: Jastrow

THE NEXT OBSTACLE – CRETE AND TALOS

There is considerable debate as to who, or indeed what, Talos was. It is generally agreed that he was a gigantic bronze-clad being in the shape of a man. (Some ancient myths argue for the shape of a bull, but this is probably because the culture of Knossos is inextricably linked with bulls.) Many believed that Talos was a relic of a previous era – the Age of Bronze.

The humans of the Heroic Age were not the first attempt at producing the species. Various proto-humans had existed beforehand, including the dreamy flower-children of the Golden Age. These men (women had not yet been invented) lived long, useless lives before being replaced by the people of the Silver Age whom Zeus destroyed because they failed to give due honour to the gods. Next up were the men of the Bronze Age – a breed conceived from the hard wood of the ash tree who lived for only for war and destruction. So terrible were the men of the Bronze Age and so great the chaos of their wars that Zeus eventually destroyed that batch also and thereafter gave up on the business of creating humans. This is possibly why he was so peeved when Prometheus created the humans of the Heroic Age, a species which generally succeeded where the King of the Gods had failed.

Yet one survivor remained of the Age of Bronze, and Talos was he. Zeus appreciated the creature's talent for destruction, and set him to guard the island of Crete, for he had stashed there the beautiful Europa, a princess whom he had kidnapped and wanted to keep safe from jealous Hera. Even with Europa gone Talos still tirelessly patrolled the island, circling its shores three times every day to keep the inhabitants safe from harm. Should any unauthorized ship appear on the horizon Talos would hurl huge boulders at it until the ship either retreated from the barrage or was crushed beneath the massive missiles.

Others argued that Talos was no bronze-age relic but an automaton forged by the cunning craftsmanship of Hephaestus and gifted to Minos. Those proposing this theory pointed out that if survivors of Talos' boulder-induced shipwreck managed to struggle ashore, Talos was in the habit of lying in the nearest fire until his armour became red hot. He would then pull his victims into a devastating hug which ensured that they were crushed and sear-roasted at the same time. If there was really a human inside the armour, point out the automaton-theorists, than that human would have baked himself at the same time as his victim.

Furthermore, Talos did not have the same circulatory system as humans. Rather than blood he was powered by ichor – that same divine substance as ran in the veins of the gods. In the case of Talos there was but a single vein which ran from one ankle to his neck. As further proof that Talos was some form of infernal engine, it was pointed out that the vein holding the ichor was stopped by a single nail at the ankle.

This nail was used also by Greek craftsmen when casting statues in bronze. Because bronze cannot be chiselled away like marble, a sculptor would make his creation from wax. Then the waxen statue would be covered in clay apart from a single hole in the ankle which was stopped with a nail. The clay was baked in a furnace until it became ceramic and the wax was liquefied. The nail would then be removed and the wax would flow out. Thereafter the empty mould would be refilled with molten bronze which, as it solidified, would take the shape of the lost wax figure. Shatter the ceramic, and lo! The result would be a bronze statue somewhat resembling the mighty Talos.

The final argument that Talos was a machine rather than a homicidal human relic of an earlier era was based on another rather odd habit of his. During his circuits of Crete Talos would regularly detour to different villages on a schedule that took him to each settlement every four months. Once there he would show to the villagers several bronze plates which he always carried with him. Upon these were inscribed the laws of the island. None other than the philosopher Plato testifies to this.

Three times a year Talos went around the villages, preserving their laws by holding them engraved on tablets of bronze.

Plato *Minos* 320c

Written laws were something of a radical development in Greece, and that remained so even centuries later. Without written laws, most cases were decided by judges who pretty much made up the law as they went along. This led to marked differences in verdicts (consider the feelings of those who came up before a certain judge called Draco. He once remarked, 'The penalty for even minor infringements should be death and I cannot think of anything more severe for worse cases', thus giving us the modern term 'draconian punishments'). Nor did it help that judges were generally members of the local elite and when it came to court cases they naturally tended to favour members of their own social group.

Therefore having written laws which people could see for themselves and which the judges were required to follow and enforce was seen as a radical and populist move. It was certainly not the kind of thing which a ravening killer from an age of anarchic violence might be expected to promote. On the other hand, if Talos were indeed a creation of the craftsman god Hephaestus, that is exactly what he would do. Hephaestus had considerable sympathy for the underdog, being something of an underdog himself.

All of this was somewhat academic to the Argonauts, since their unheralded approach to Crete introduced them not to Talos the civilized lawman, but to Talos the boulder-hurling vigilante. Fortunately the *Argo* was nimbler than most ships and the Argonauts were extremely practised rowers. Nevertheless, as the *Argo* wove its way shoreward with ever-closer fountains of water erupting on each side, Jason was finally forced to admit that Talos' aim was improving to the point where the *Argo* would eventually be hit and sunk. Reluctantly he ordered the crew to back water until they were safely out of range.

The problem was that the Argonauts were counting on a landfall in Crete to restock on water and supplies after their exhausting journey from North Africa. They had neither the food, water nor energy to take their ship elsewhere at short notice and now it seemed that they also could not approach the only haven within reach. There was a very real danger that their mission would come to an ignominious end right there, with the ship stranded at sea just out of range of Talos' artillery.

It was time for the Argonauts to unleash their wea-

THE NEXT OBSTACLE – CRETE AND TALOS

pon of last resort - Medea. Putting Medea into play meant that someone was certain to die, but since that someone was probably Talos, the exasperated Argonauts could not bring themselves to feel much regret.

Medea herself showed no doubt in her abilities, confidently addressing the Argonauts. 'Okay, listen to me. Unless he is totally immortal, I can take this creature down on my own, even if he is wearing armour or is solid bronze throughout. Just keep the ship out of his range until I am on top of things.'

There are different accounts of how Medea accomplished her task because the story of Medea and Talos is very ancient – older even than the legend of Jason and the Argonauts. Some of the stories can be dismissed as 'doublets' – that it, re-tellings of Medea's previous or future exploits adapted to the present situation. Others are less likely doublets than Medea deploying tried and trusted techniques. The version given below is a synthesis of the different accounts arranged in the manner which seems most credible. First, Medea would have prepared a censer filled with opiates and ordered one of the Argonauts to ignite the contents when instructed to do so.

This done, it was time to tackle the most obvious issue facing Medea at the outset, namely that she had to get into spell-casting range beneath Talos' bombardment of rocks. For this she needed allies, and as a student of dread Hecate, Medea naturally sought these allies from the Underworld. The Argonauts shrank back in dread as Medea crouched in the stern of the ship, pulling her purple robe close about her cheeks, singing and chanting in supplication as dark forces swirled about her.

Only the most skilled of witches would dare to invoke the powers which Medea now called to her aid. These were the Keres, the death-spirits, the eaters of life, the demonic beings known as the 'hounds of Hades'. In fact, the Keres were not canine but semi-human winged figures in female form who wore robes soaked in human blood. The Greeks personified death as Thanatos, the grim reaper who plucked souls from their bodies as they passed away. Yet Thanatos operated mainly where people died peacefully. When it came to violent death in battle, murder or plague, the Keres got there first. The Keres fed upon the energies released at the moment of death and their insatiable hunger drew them in flocks to the battlefield where they ripped the souls from warriors, sometimes before the wounded bodies could hit the ground.

Homer describes a scene in which one such spirit 'drags a corpse by his feet through the carnage. The shoulders of her dress are saturated with blood, and she glares wildly and gnashes her teeth as the other Keres fight and yank away from one another the bodies of the fallen.' *Iliad* **18.540**

The problem with calling up spirits hungry for blood and death was that the summoner needed to supply both in a hurry, because the Keres would not return to the Underworld unsated. In other words, once Medea had invoked the Keres, they *would* feed - either upon Talos or upon Medea herself. In the battle to make landfall, Medea had now drastically raised the stakes.

Medea had summoned the Keres and thus put herself into their power, but Talos was not vulnerable to the demonic entities in the same way. (Given the

THE NEXT OBSTACLE – CRETE AND TALOS

insatiable hunger of the Keres, life on earth would rapidly become extinct if they could do their own killing.) Yet this was only Medea's first step. While the Keres could not kill Talos, they could confuse and blind the creature, and this they proceeded to do.

As soon as Medea was sure that her invocation had succeeded and Talos was effectively blinded, she signalled that it was now safe for the Argonauts to bring their ship to shore. As the *Argo* grounded on the beach Medea rose from the stern and climbed down onto the sand, still chanting and singing. But now she had changed her tone from the shrill chants of her invocation to a gentle, soothing lullaby. In this manner she neared the giant bronze figure, approaching from upwind so that the breeze carried the scent of soporific herbs from the censer she had prepared earlier. Medea probably reasoned that Talos may or may not be a species of human. If he was, then the herbs would further serve to stultify him. If he was simply a robot the fumes would be wasted but they could certainly not hinder Medea's plans.

Singing softly, Medea came to stand beside the bewildered and blinded Talos. With soothing words as beguiling as a politician's promise she assured him that everything was going to be all right. Talos would feel just one quick pinch and he would be restored to his power. Better yet, if he were not immortal, Medea's treatment would make him so. Medea's soft hypnotic chants slowly soothed the agitation of Talos until the giant bronze figure stood still and submitted to her ministrations. One quick pinch was indeed all he felt as Medea deftly plucked out the nail which stopped the vein running from his ankle to his neck. As soon as the life-force of Talos began to run from his body into the sand the Keres pounced upon their victim and mighty Talos was doomed.

So Talos, formidable as was his bronze frame, nevertheless was defeated by the sorceress Medea. ... The ichor poured out like molten lead and he could remain standing no longer. It was as with a tall pine high in the mountains, which the woodsmen have cut half-through their sharp axes before returning [home] *from the forest. At first the tree merely shudders in the night winds, but finally it snaps at the trunk and comes crashing down. In exactly this manner Talos remained on his untiring feet, shivering back and forth, until at last his strength failed and his body toppled to smite the earth.*

Argonautica 1675ff.

Talos was vanquished, but this hardly made Crete a safe haven for the Argonauts. While the man of bronze had been a life-threatening danger to the Argonauts, he was something of a hero to the people of Crete. They would not look kindly upon the travellers who had killed off their protector, so it was probably best of Medea passed up the opportunity to pay her respects to aunt Pasiphae. In their own way Minos and Pasiphae were every bit as formidable as Aeëtes and Circe, with the major difference that the latter two did not have a cannibalistic child in constant need of fresh meat.

Therefore the Argonauts deemed it best not to tell the royal couple that they had destroyed Talos in the process of making landfall on Crete. In fact, they felt that it would be best that they re-stocked their ship and left the island so speedily that they could plausibly

THE NEXT OBSTACLE – CRETE AND TALOS

deny that they had ever been there in the first place, yet alone met Talos. Consequently, their brief time on Crete was more like a clandestine commando raid than the royal parade of some of their other Mediterranean island visits.

Once they had refilled their water-skins and probably left several local peasants bewildered by the sudden disappearance of their chickens and goats, the Argonauts hurriedly set sail once more. They deemed it so urgent that they should leave before someone discovered the remains of Talos stretched out on the sand that they defied conventional nautical wisdom and literally slipped away like thieves into the night.

There was a reason why sea travel was generally a daytime activity in the ancient world, and this had to do with the lack of a compass. The open sea is remarkably free of any landmarks, which makes it difficult to determine in which direction the vagaries of wind and current are carrying the ship. The obvious answer would be to keep near the coast, were it not for the fact that the land does not conveniently end at the water's edge. Rather it has a nasty habit of carrying on for some distance just beneath the waves in the form of semi-submerged rocks, shoals and sandbanks, all of which are hard to see in the dark.

In any case, the Argonauts did not have the option of hugging the coast as their intention was to put that coast as far behind them as possible before sunrise. The next option therefore would be to take a sighting on the pole star, or rather upon the gap between the stars Ursa Minor alpha and beta in a chain of stars which the Greeks called the 'Dog's Tail'. This, they knew, was the one unchanging point about which the heavens wheeled overhead through the night and so provided the means to set a course.

Unless the sky was at it was at this time - overcast and the night so unrelievedly black that it was impossible to even see the line where sea and sky divided, let alone discern the finer points required for celestial navigation. After a while no-one on the *Argo* was sure whether the ship floated in the waters off the coast of Crete, upon the blacker waters of Hades, or some place in between. At this point a somewhat over-stressed Jason broke into tears and promised sacrifices to Apollo at Delphi, at Delos and at every other place sacred to the god if he would just give them a sign.

Obligingly, Apollo dropped a meteorite through the clouds so that it appeared as a brief streak, a golden arrow shooting above the sea. Before this divine intervention vanished from sight the weary sailors glimpsed the peaks of a mountainous island not far off, and this they made for in a hurry. The island was bare and desolate, but it was a secure anchorage where the Argonauts could wait as the clouds rolled back and the dawn brought a bright sunrise. The travellers put to sea that day with a sense of renewed optimism.

An interesting digression takes place at this point. One of the Argonauts had become a particular friend of the sea-god Triton while the *Argo* was struggling to escape from his lake on the shores of North Africa. When the ship had reached the open sea once more, Triton had given the Argonaut a farewell present - a clod of earth which he called an 'island seed'. Now, with the *Argo* making good speed towards the Greek mainland, it occurred to the sailor that the clod of earth should either be used immediately or not at all. (After their maritime adventures, not a few Argonauts were determined never to so much as set eyes upon salt water ever again.)

Fruit of the island seed: Santorini today

Accordingly, the Argonaut consulted with Jason who agreed in a spirit of scientific enquiry that they should drop the clod overboard and watch what happened. What happened is that an island appeared above the waves, like a broaching whale but hundreds of times larger. This island the Argonauts called Calliste, but in later years it came to be called Thera. Thera (modern Santorini) does indeed lie between Crete and mainland Greece, and being volcanic – it was to erupt spectacularly in 1600 BC – it may well have arisen from the waves as described.

However archaeology shows that the island was

settled in what was, even for Jason and his Argonauts, the distant past. Thus while the story of Jason's Argonauts as island creators is decidedly wrong, it may be that preserved in the story of Jason and Medea are the last echoes of folk tales from those primitive people who did in fact see the emergence of Thera from the sea thousands and thousands of years before.

The good ship *Argo* now made speedy progress across the waters of the Aegean Sea. Before long the ship was anchored in the friendly waters of Aegina, just off the coast of mainland Greece. Local village youths helped the Argonauts carry vases of water to the ship, and soon this developed into a spirited competition. This, allegedly is the source of a tradition which continued through much of antiquity where athletic events upon the island of Aegina uniquely featured a race with runners carrying water-jars.

From there the *Argo* crossed the Saronic gulf, and Medea got her first glimpse of Athens – which was not yet the capital it would become of a unified city-state, but simply the largest of a diverse group of towns and villages newly merged into the political entity of Attica. Then followed a gentle cruise through the channel between the island of Euboea and the mainland, with the kingdom of Iolcus just over the horizon.

By now the mood of the Argonauts was one of delighted relief. These were home waters and while in the Heroic Age nowhere in Greece was completely safe, Jason's band of adventurers felt reasonably capable of handling whatever hazards the local environment could throw at them. As the *Argo* neared journey's end the only persons aboard who might have felt more apprehension than relief were Jason and Medea.

THE NEXT OBSTACLE – CRETE AND TALOS

Having obtained the Fleece, the rest of the crew would return home with a fine stock of tales to tell and their heroic reputations assured. For Jason though, arrival in Iolcus marked only a further step in his journey to remove the land's usurper king and restore his father to the throne. Exactly how he was going to accomplish this was uncertain, especially as he now had at his side Medea, which was the equivalent of bringing a flame-thrower to a diplomatic discussion.

Medea herself was probably as apprehensive as someone with her supreme self-assurance could get. She was, after all, going from a land where she was a princess to one where she was a supplicant dependent upon her husband's goodwill. Furthermore she had probably already worked out from the reaction of the Argonauts to her brand of dark magic that her mere presence aroused considerable anxiety in bystanders. As a protege of Hecate in Colchis she had been respected, almost venerated. In her new homeland it seemed that she was more likely to inspire horror mixed with a large dollop of sheer terror.

Of course, this might help Jason by giving him a degree of leverage in the coming delicate negotiations about the royal succession in Iolcus. However, before anyone feared Medea, they had to know her. If the slight, introspective Medea looked and acted like any other new bride in Greece, she would accordingly be treated as such by the casually misogynistic society in which she was about to find herself. Unless she revealed her powers, Medea was more likely to be overlooked than feared.

A bride was a mere appendage of her husband - a vehicle for passing his inheritance on to the next generation. Would the royal court of Iolcus take a brief look at Medea and judge that reports of her abilities were no more than exaggerated traveller's tales? Would anyone take her seriously?

In short, were the rulers of Iolcus about to make a gigantic mistake?

Chapter 7

Dark Deeds in Iolcus

As a princess of Colchis, Medea was aware that being a monarch was not all about cheering subjects and royal banquets. In her time a king had to work extremely hard to keep his crown, and even harder to keep the head upon which that crown sat. The world was filled with heroes and demi-gods who might take lethal umbrage against a king or who might fancy ruling the kingdom themselves (Hercules alone dispatched some half-a-dozen kings to the Underworld). Furthermore, while the gods paid little attention to ordinary folk they were rather interested in the doings of royalty, who, given the frequent interbreeding of gods and humans, were often also relatives. Being smitten by divine wrath was no uncommon cause of royal deaths and even kings whom the gods favoured could run into trouble as a result (King Midas being an excellent example).

As well as problems with erratic, feuding and arbitrary gods there were the usual dynastic issues which have plagued royalty ever since the institution was invented. Combine all these and the result was the sort of poisonous mixture which an interested Medea discovered in Iolcus – namely a long-running and often lethal drama of operatic proportions.

In earlier chapters the relationship of Jason with his uncle, the current king of Iolcus has been touched upon, and doubtless the long voyage on the *Argo* had given Jason plenty of time to get his wife familiar with the general outline of how things stood with his dysfunctional family. Nevertheless, now that Jason was about to plunge once more into the scorpion-pit of dynastic politics, Medea set about doing her own research. She discovered a convoluted tale, the essence of which is given below.

The family's problems started with Tyro of Iolcus, wife to the then monarch Cretheus. Despite being queen in a modestly thriving city-state and the mother of three sons, Tyro was unhappy. Secretly she lusted after one Enipus, a minor deity who personified a local river of the same name. (This river is now the river Enipeas in Thessaly, famous as the site where Caesar later defeated Pompey at Pharsalus in 48 BC).

The river-god Enipus was sensible enough to want nothing to do with the amorous Tyro, so the unfaithful queen was rather surprised when he abruptly succumbed to her advances. She was even more surprised when she discovered that her lover was not Enipus but Poseidon who had adopted the form of the lesser god to enjoy a bit of casual sex. Tyro was even more surprised still to discover that her liaison had caused her to become pregnant with twins.

What followed was standard stuff for those who follow such events. Tyro, like many women in the ancient world, practised what has been brutally described as 'post-natal birth control'. That is, once the children were born, she took them to a local mountain and abandoned them there to die, in much the same way as royal children were abandoned in baskets in rivers (Moses, Romulus and Remus, Sargon the Great) then later found and adopted by shepherds (Romulus and Remus, Cyrus the Great, Oedipus). The twins raised by the shepherd on this occasion were named Pelias and Neleus.

Exactly why children abandoned in this way should feel any great sympathy for their mother is uncertain, but Pelias and Neleus apparently did. Once grown to man's estate they gathered a rebel force and took power in Iolcus. Or rather Pelias did, for once he had no further need for Neleus, that unfortunate brother was politically isolated and promptly exiled from the kingdom.

Earth-shaking Poseidon, Lord of the Sea and father of Pelias of Iolcus

What became of the previous king is unknown, but the fate of his wife is highly relevant to our tale. Cretheus had renounced Tyro once she became pregnant by Poseidon and remarried. His new wife was a woman called Sidero, a worshipper of Hera who brutally mistreated Tyro once she had power over her. When he took over the kingdom Pelias hunted down Sidero, eventually finding her where she had taken sanctuary in a temple of Hera, and he killed her there. Thereafter, aware that he had earned Hera's undying enmity for his impious deed, Pelias made no attempt to appease the goddess, relying instead on the protection of his father Poseidon. (Once freed from Sidero's brutality Tyro left Iolcus and went on to marry one Sisyphus, another king who fell out with the gods and ended up eternally rolling a boulder up a hill in the Underworld.)

Pelias also exiled his half-brothers, the children of King Cretheus and Tyro, but decided to keep a close eye on their eldest son who was the legitimate heir to the throne of Iolcus. This was Aeson, the father of Jason. Pelias had kept Aeson imprisoned in Iolcus, presumably on the grounds that while he kept the legitimate heir to the throne in his power none of the other family members had a claim to the kingdom. This worked well for a long time until the appearance of Jason, the son whom Pelias never realized that Aeson had. For a while though, it seemed that Pelias had warded off danger here also by sending Jason off to Colchis on a suicide mission from which he had not returned.

Except now he had, bringing with him the Golden Fleece which signified his right to kingship and also bringing home with him a shy young wife - of whom the boatload of battle-hardened heroes from the *Argo* appeared to be inexplicably terrified. Suddenly the crown of Pelias was wobbling.

Pelias was nothing if not decisive. Right now, Jason was the hero of the hour and so was untouchable. Jason's parents and a younger son born to them during Jason's absence were less so, and Pelias quickly disposed of them. He murdered the son and the mother committed suicide. (The order of these events is uncertain.) There is considerably more confusion about what became of Aeson, who was old and frail by this time anyway. By one account Aeson foresaw his fate and killed himself. By other reports, Pelias killed him along with the rest of his family. (In a final version it was Medea who did the deed, apparently to clear the way for Jason's succession.)

A cynic might look at the latter case and note how convenient it would be for Pelias if Aeson were to die – thus removing one rival – and the blame for the murder be attached to Medea, thus discrediting another rival - Jason - for bringing home a barbarian wife who already had two impressive kills against her name. As to Medea herself, well, the woman hardly mattered. She was a mere slip of a girl who could take the blame for this political killing simply because of her overblown reputation. Overall, Pelias could pat himself on the back for a some smart, albeit bloody, political manoeuvring.

It is uncertain exactly how Aeson met his death because sadly at this point Medea's story takes leave of the narrator who has given the account of Medea's adventures ever since Jason's arrival in Colchis.

Apollonius Rhodius was interested in telling the story of the travels of the *Argo* and its crew, and once the good ship was safely docked in Iolcus, Apollonius Rhodius brought his story to an end. His *Argonautica* now ceases to be a guide and the *Fabulae* of Hyginus and the *Metamorphoses* of the Roman poet Ovid take up the tale.

In Ovid's version, Aeson was alive but at death's door when the Argonauts returned. The parents of the various heroes gathered in Iolcus to celebrate the return of their sons with a huge party, including sacrifices of sheep and cattle and the melting of incense in the flames of the fire upon which the victims were roasted. Yet absent from the general rejoicing was Aeson 'now worn out from his long life and fast approaching death'. Or, as already discussed, it may have been that Pelias had already killed Aeson and framed Medea.

Crying without restraint, Jason now turned to his wife and said,

'Medea, I admit I owe you my life - and almost everything else - because of what you have done for me. Though your goodness to me is beyond anything that you had promised, can your magics do one thing more for me? (And I now believe they can do almost anything.) Please, take some of the years from my own lifespan, and add them to my father's.'

Medea was moved by the plea, not least because she contrasted the bond Jason shared with his father with her own abandonment by and of Aeëtes. Nevertheless, she knew that she could not allow herself to be moved by his plea, and answered. 'Husband, don't talk

of forbidden things. Even if I could give a part of someone's life to another, you should not ask me to do it, and Hecate would not let me if I tried. Yet there is another way which will give what you ask, and that without taking years from your own life. It involves great risk and I must ask in person for the Triple Goddess to give her assent to the rite, but yes, I can make the attempt to extend your father's life.'

Metamorphoses 7.159ff

Apparently unconcerned about the 'great risk' (which Jason would not personally be taking) our hero beseeched Medea to get on with it.

Medea could not immediately 'get on with it' because she needed to work her conjurations beneath a full moon and the next one was still a few days off. In the meantime she used the herbs and unguents in her pharmacopoeia to put Jason's father into a state of suspended animation.

Then while her patient hovered between life and death Medea had to wait until the third day and the dead of night 'when men, birds and beasts were deep asleep, there was no movement in the dew-filled air and only the sparkling stars moved in the heavens.' (Says Ovid) Then Medea left the palace in her bare feet, with her robes untied and her hair hanging loose. This attire itself tells of the danger of her mission.

The Roman poet Ovid is now telling the tale, and in Roman tradition when one comes into the presence of evil spirits they can catch hold of any fastening, knot or buckle on the wearer's clothing or hair and while so attached work their malign will upon their victim. That Medea dared not even risk the strap on a sandal indicates that she was venturing into dangerous territory indeed.

By way of further purification Medea three times washed her head with water from a fast-moving stream (supernatural beings prefer still water – as shown even today in the belief that vampires cannot cross running water). Three times she turned to free herself of any ghostly beings who might cling to her and then, as free from taint as she could be, Medea uttered the long, wailing cry by which she summoned her ride.

The heroes of the *Argo* might have become somewhat indignant at this point. Once they had committed to Jason's quest there was no turning back for them. They had perforce to endure monstrous attacks, towering seas, exotic, homicidal monsters and the constant threat of death on all sides with no choice but to battle through all of it if they were ever to arrive safely back home. Now, with none of these heroes to observe, Medea demonstrated that through all those perilous adventures, she had only been along for the ride. She could have bailed out at any time.

Now summoned, Medea's potential lifeboat from the *Argo* dropped like a shooting star from the heavens and settled gently on the dewy grass beside her. It was a golden chariot - without wheels because it was not designed to travel upon the earth. Even asking for that would be an insult to the shining dragons which pulled the chariot, their wings now folded and heads bowed as they awaited Medea's command.

The sorceress gently stroked the necks of her fearsome pets and then gathered their reins as she mounted the chariot. One shake of those reins and she was snatched into the heavens from where she could behold the kingdom of Iolcus as an insignificant speck on the edge of the Thessalian plain spread out far below her.

Her journey was to take nine days and nine nights - not because her dragons were slow, and not because the herbs she needed were scattered across distant locations - though they were - but because to be properly efficacious, some herbs have to be gathered by the light of a full moon, some others three nights later, and some three times three (i.e. nine) nights later. Most of the herbs grew on inaccessible ledges and ridges of remote mountains, such as Mt Pelion (in south-eastern Thessaly, elevation 1,624 meters), Mt Pindus (technically a mountain range between Greece and Albania, elevation 2,037 m) Mt Olympus (2,432m and known even today for its diverse and abundant flora) and Mt Othrys (where stray magic from ancient warfare between the Olympian gods and the Titans had caused strange plants to bloom).

Then the rivers of Hellas were plundered of exotic plants, all carefully cut with a bronze sickle. (Iron was known but rare, but in any case cutting with an iron blade would destroy the magical properties of many of the herbs Medea had come so far to gather.) Yet none of these rare and exotic plants were needed to restore life to Aeson. Jason's father could actually be revived by a single application of the innocent-looking sheaf of grass which Medea gathered from beside a spring on Mt Oreia. The other materials were needed to counter the side-effects of that application, which included bodily deformity and madness, not to mention the gruesome fate of ever ageing, but never dying. (A fisherman called Glaucus was to discover this the hard way a generation later.)

Nor was the cure totally vegetarian. A screech owl – an ill-omened bird sacred to Hades - went into the mix, along with the slavered drool gathered from the jaws of a female werewolf (how *that* was collected should be worth a myth in itself). The skin of a water-snake, the liver of a stag and the head and eggs of a crow were all part of the infernal recipe. Even uncombined, the scented ingredients of the potion affected the dragons who drew Medea's chariot through the skies. Being magical creatures themselves, they were particularly susceptible to magic, and now their skins split and sloughed off, revealing gleaming new scales beneath.

Her dark materials assembled, Medea turned for home. Her work was far from done and still she had to work alone, for exactly the same reason that a modern chemist does not allow amateurs to prepare nitroglycerine. First, in a space open to the sky Medea had to construct two altars, one to Hebe, the goddess of youth and one to Hecate, the goddess whose magical influence would act as catalyst to the entire conjuration. Linking the two altars, Medea dug a shallow trench.

Once all this was set up, the body of Aeson was carried to the scene by attendants who could hardly leave the scene fast enough once they were dismissed. To begin the ritual Medea dragged forth a black sheep and slit its throat, carefully positioning the animal so that its blood drained into the trenches. (Black sheep seem to have been particularly important in raising the dead. We see Odysseus later performing a similar rite in *Odyssey* 10.504–540 &

11.23-50 and Orestes at his father's grave in the *Electra* of Euripides 91-92.)

Then Medea lit fires on both altars and – still with hair and clothing unbound – lit multi-branched torches from the flames which she then extinguished by plunging them into the pools of blood. Next she turned to her unconscious patient and purified him, three times with fire, three times with water, and three times with sulphur. All the while on the bare earth between the altars a huge cauldron bubbled and seethed as Medea's painstakingly gathered materials boiled within. Eventually the heated mixture spat forth gobbets of white froth and where these hit the ground, the once bare earth immediately burst into bloom with flowers and deep, soft grass. Observing this, Medea picked up her stirrer - an ancient olive branch - and gave the pot a solid stirring. She withdrew the branch and tossed it aside once it became useless for its purpose, being now covered in fresh green leaves and laden with olives.

Now for the critical bit. Gently, Medea drew the old man toward her and carefully revived him from the coma into which he had been placed. It was just as well that Jason had been banished from the ritual as one can only imagine his reaction as his father returned to consciousness just in time to see a smiling Medea lean forward with her knife. Before her horrified victim could utter his first terrified scream Medea had slit his throat from ear-to-ear and stepped back to watch his feeble death-struggles.

Even before the body had stopped twitching Medea had drawn a ladle of her potion from the frothing cauldron and poured it directly into Aeson through the gaping wound in this throat. She stopped when the wound closed, and forced the man to absorb more of the potion by pouring it into his mouth. The struggles of the old man ceased and became the struggles of a young man. Colour flowed back into his age-whitened hair and beard, muscles wasted with age plumped out as the deep hollows of his cheeks and eyes were replaced with rounded flesh.

Within minutes where once an old man had lain, his spirit already most of the way through death's door, there now reclined a man four decades younger. Aeson was again in the prime of his years, his mouth agape with wonder as he felt the long-forgotten strength of youth surging through his body. Medea's rejuvenation treatment had been an unqualified success.

There could be no doubt henceforth as to the efficacy of Medea's magic. Aeson was back on his feet, hailed by the old men of the kingdom who immediately recognized the companion of their youth. What became of Aeson thereafter is unknown as further dramatic events swept his personal story into oblivion even as Medea's fame spread. Word of the miraculous restoration reached as far as Mt Olympus and soon the kingdom was abuzz with the news that that the great god Dionysus had beseeched Medea to share her potion so that he might reward the ageing nymphs who had cared for him as a baby. Indeed it seemed that the only person unimpressed by Medea's amazing feat was Jason himself.

The cause of the quarrel between the lovebirds is uncertain, though some have speculated that their problems arose because Jason wanted Medea to revive his mother also. Medea demurred because the mother had been dead too long for a successful reanimation and besides, having taken the extreme risks involved in the ritual once, Medea would really rather not do it again. The more that Jason insisted that Medea should make the attempt, the more stubbornly Medea refused. Matters finally escalated into a screaming match that ended only when Medea stormed out of the marital home.

Unsurprisingly, although Medea had arrived in Iolcus as an unwanted nobody, it seemed that everyone now wanted to be her friend and offers of hospitality poured in. Pushing aside all the other claimants to Medea's company were the daughters of King Pelias himself. Claiming royal privilege, they speedily 'rescued the supplicant Medea' and escorted her to the palace. Jason meanwhile absented himself from Iolcus to sail the *Argo* to a new berth in Corinth.

Of course, the daughters of Pelias wanted for their father what Jason had wanted for his mother. The difference was that Pelias was not recently dead – as Aeson might have been – or about to die (though Medea had some plans in that direction). Instead Pelias was old but healthy – an ideal candidate for Medea's magic if she could be persuaded to use it. It is not hard to see how Medea might have won the friendship of the daughters. She had a huge stock of tales, both of exotic Colchis and first-hand experience of the adventures of the Argonauts. Medea might also have taught the young women some basic magic tricks and then flattered them that they were natural magical practitioners.

On the subject of rejuvenating Pelias though, Medea

was much more reluctant. Her very hesitancy made the daughters even more enthusiastic and they begged Medea to set her price, however great it might be. It may have helped that Medea had still some of the ingredients from her previous concoction and had no need to start gathering materials from scratch. (The werewolf might have been particularly averse to being revisited.) Eventually, Medea was prevailed upon to at least demonstrate how she might rejuvenate Pelias. After all, now that Jason was hostile toward her, the daughters argued that Medea would benefit greatly from the gratitude of Pelias and the longer the king lived, the longer he could protect her.

So Medea prepared a demonstration which was also partly an experiment to see how her materials had endured in the time since they had been gathered. Again the altars were prepared and again the fire was lit beneath the bronze cauldron. The experimental animal on this occasion was a ram, the oldest of the sheep in the royal flocks. 'The horns of the woolly beast curved deep around its hollowed forehead and it was barely able to struggle as it was brought forward, so advanced were its years. The creature had blood so thin that it barely marked the blade which Medea drew across its age-withered throat', Ovid tells us as the ritual reached its climactic moment.

At this point the tales diverge. Ovid relates that Medea then plunged the carcass entire into the cauldron. Others say that first she rent the beast limb from limb and chopped the torso into pieces, claiming that this would allow the potion to reach all the parts of the animal at once. Either way the horrified sisters watched as the mass of flesh was submerged within the foaming liquid of the cauldron. Seconds passed as the horns and limbs of the ram melted away, and with them the long years of the creature's existence. Abruptly the awed silence was broken by high-pitched bleats, and while the spectators were searching for the origins of the sound, a lamb leapt from the cauldron. It stood for a moment and then gambolled away looking for mother and milk, while the daughters of Pelias watched its departure in stunned silence.

Medea's Ram revival as shown on this late archaic Athenian red-figure vase

Once they had seen what the cauldron could do there was no stopping the daughters. Pelias should be rejuvenated, and that very evening. The daughters announced that they had endured Medea's prevarications and teasing long enough. It was time to give their father the surprise of his life. (By some other versions of this ancient legend, Medea performed her demonstration before Pelias himself, so the proceedings may not have come as so much of a shock as Ovid suggests.) Medea was able to put off their urgent imprecations, but for three days only. She insisted she needed that time to recharge her stock of herbs and to refresh the contents of the cauldron.

On the fourth night a small group converged upon the king's sleeping quarters. The king was within, deep in slumber. It would not have surprised anyone who knew Medea that the king's bodyguards were likewise deep asleep, so the little group entered the royal bedchamber unchallenged. The women stood around Pelias with daggers drawn, but it is hard for a loving daughter to stab her father, no matter how benign her intentions. A long, hesitant silence followed, which was broken by Medea who remarked, 'Well now it is up to you. Either you want your father rejuvenated or you do not. It is in your hands whether or not the old blood is drained from his body and replaced with the invigorating potion – if you want to cure him of old age you must do so with the points of your daggers.'

Since none of the daughters could bring themselves to strike the first blow Medea organized a synchronized strike whereby all three would plunge their daggers into their sleeping father at the same time.

DARK DEEDS IN IOLCUS

This did not work quite as well as intended because none of the women could bear to witness their own act and all struck blindly with their heads averted. As a result Pelias was severely lacerated, streaming with blood, alive and very much awake. He pulled his bleeding body upright and stretched out his arms to his children. 'My daughters! What have I done that has driven you to murder the father who believed that you loved him? Can you ...'.

Pelias got no further because, once it was clear that the daughters had lost the will to continue with their lethal enterprise, Medea concluded the conversation by drawing her blade across Pelias' throat. Now forced upon their course, the daughters carried their father's corpse past the slumbering guards to the cauldron which was already frothing busily. According to Ovid – whom we have mostly followed to this point – Medea then dumped the body into the boiling water. In an alternative tradition followed by several other ancient authors (e.g. Apollodurus *Bibliotheca* 1.9.27), Medea insisted that the daughters should first convert Pelias into mincemeat all the better for the potion to reach the king's constituent parts.

The daughters grimly went through the process of butchering their father's body and doubtless felt huge relief when they were finally able to place the bloody remains into the seething waters of the cauldron. Then they stepped back and waited with breathless expectation for their father's return. And waited ... and waited. Finally when the delay became intolerable, the daughters turned desperately to Medea to urgently enquire what was going on – but Medea was not there. At some point in the proceedings she had quietly slipped away, and no-one was better than she at departing unseen. The daughters were left clinging to the fast-receding hope that their father would return from the soup, but already they were beginning to come to terms with the realization that they had been duped. Pelias had been murdered and they had been the unwitting instruments of his death.

Pelias with his wife and a daughter from a 1st century AD Roman fresco

In many ways it was the perfect murder. The king's daughters could hardly deny their involvement – their daggers had done the deed, and their blood-splattered clothing provided eloquent testimony to their guilt. Medea on the other hand had passed in and out of the king's chambers unnoticed and her fatal cut had been done too neatly to stain her clothes. She could credibly deny ever having been there. Meanwhile Jason – with whom Medea was about to become 'reconciled' - had been out of Iolcus the entire time taking the *Argo* to its new berth and would be making his planned return just in time to hear the tragic news.

Ideally, the daughters would realize that their position was indefensible and they would quietly make their father's stewed corpse disappear. Alternatively, without going into the gruesome details, they could proclaim that their tyrannous father had perished in a palace coup and then hail Jason as the new king. Either way, Medea had good reason to believe that she was about to become ensconced as queen of Iolcus. Not bad going, for a refugee girl from Colchis.

Chapter 8

A Different World
Greece in the Heroic Age

For once Medea had miscalculated. She had assumed that after she had manipulated the daughters of Pelias into killing their father they would have only two options – to conceal the body and their own guilt or to come brazenly forward and admit that they had assassinated a tyrannical parent in order to clear the way for Jason. This might cause a short-term scandal, but in an era of brutal palace politics it was not unusual for kings to come to a sticky end (or a gooey one in the case of Pelias).

Medea might have had in mind that perfect example of a dysfunctional Greek royal family, the infamous house of Atreus. This dynasty was founded by Tantalus, who fed his son Pelops to the Greek gods at a banquet and was punished by being forever tantalized in the Underworld by food and drink just out of his reach. Restored to life, Pelops went on to become king by killing his rival. The sons of Pelops contended for the throne of Mycenae (after the children of Hercules had killed the current occupant) in a struggle that included rape, cannibalism, bestiality, incest, suicide, fratricide, and general murder. In the coming generation the father would literally sacrifice his daughter, his wife would kill him and their son would kill the mother in response.

Given such circumstances, Medea might justifiably have reckoned that the death of Pelias would be considered a relatively normal event in the rough-and-tumble of contemporary politics. Pelias himself had taken the throne by force, killed a woman of the previous dynasty in a temple of Hera, and worked hard to kill off as many of Jason's family as he could. Arguably, Medea had simply got her strike in before Pelias could act against her and her husband. Jason had made a good case for being the rightful ruler when he had returned with the Fleece, and Medea had merely cleared a usurper from his path. Once Jason was on the throne of Iolcus, the original dynasty would be back in power. Everyone would forget the brief bout of preceding nastiness and that should be the end of it.

Instead Medea found that she and Jason were abused by an outraged population who heartily endorsed a different candidate for king. Jason and Medea barely got out of Iolcus without being lynched, after which the king pronounced sentence of exile upon them, declaring that their lives were forfeit should either ever set foot in the kingdom again. How could things have gone so wrong?

To answer that question it is necessary to do as Medea evidently did not, and examine the society of Greece in the Heroic age. In doing this the student of myth has an even harder task than Medea had because with the Medea myth there is also the issue of diachronicity. That is, it is generally agreed that Medea's is one of a tightly-knit group of stories that we today call 'The Greek Myths' which originated in a period somewhere around 1000 BC. Yet even at that time, the tellers of the myths set their tales in an earlier and imperfectly understood era. The resultant 'heroic age' was a mix of contemporary pre-archaic society and technology blended with earlier Bronze Age Greece.

Thus for example in the *Iliad* and other stories we see heroes riding chariots into battle in the Bronze-Age Mycenaean style. But later poets had no idea how one fights in a chariot, so when it came to the actual battle their heroes would park their vehicles and fight in a manner understood by everyone in the tenth century BC. With Medea, diachronicity means that the society in which her tale is set is an imperfect combination of how people lived in the tenth century and what was remembered of the palace-centred society of the Mycenaeans.

Nor is diachronicity an issue related only to storytelling in early Greece. For example, today we see many a film set in historical times in which the characters – especially the 'good guys' - scrupulously adhere to moral standards that would only be set centuries later. In fact our present decade has seen a rash of novels in which the female characters of Greek myth bemoan the failure of their menfolk to subscribe to the standards of the male lead in a modern Hallmark romantic movie.

In the same way much of what we know of Medea comes from ancient myths re-interpreted by writers of several later eras (e.g. classical Greece with Euripides, the later Hellenistic era for Apollonius Rhodius, and early imperial Rome for Ovid and Seneca). Each of these writers set their characters in an 'ancient' background that their contemporary audience would understand, and they often did so with a fine disregard for the details of earlier myths that had been passed down to them.

Untangling this mess is a difficult task but not an impossible one, for human nature remains a constant (which is why the ancient myths still speak to us so powerfully even today). Modern sociology and anthropology have given us the tools to understand how human nature expresses itself in different times and cultures, and generations of study have given us a better understanding of Medea's Greece and the Heroic Era.

Medea's cardinal error had been to believe that, now she and the Argonauts had returned to civilization, civilization in Hellas was the same as the one she had left behind in Colchis. In Colchis Medea had been a respected, almost feared, priestess of Hecate and a princess of the realm. While her father had been considerably embittered by her choosing the cause of Jason over his own, neither he nor anyone else had doubted Medea's capability or right to get actively involved. Indeed, almost from the moment that Jason and his heroes made landfall, one of the primary concerns of the main characters had been how to get Medea onto their side.

Therefore once Medea had fled from Colchis and arrived in Iolcus it was natural that she would update herself on local politics. That done she promptly set about changing the current situation for the benefit of herself and her spouse. This was unfortunate, as Greek society was highly unprepared for Medea's unique approach. Indeed as far as the Greeks of Iolcus were concerned, Medea had no business approaching such matters at all.

MEDEA, QUEEN OF WITCHES

Even today in the modern era we often allow our admiration of the culture and philosophical achievements of classical Greece to blind us to some of the very nasty facets of their society. And in the earlier heroic/pre-archaic era Greece was less cultured, not at all philosophical and a great deal nastier, and none of this worked in Medea's favour.

Some time around 600 BC the philosopher Thales of Miletus – generally regarded as one of the seven wisest men in Greek history – remarked, 'Three things for which I thank Fortune are; that I was born a human and not a beast, a man and not a woman, and a Greek rather than a barbarian.' These sentiments were expressed at a later time when Greece had become more tolerant, more cosmopolitan and less misogynistic than in Medea's day. Thus, while not born a beast, Medea started off in the society of Iolcus with two major strikes against her even before she stepped off the *Argo*.

She was a woman. Now, Greek males of the era would not have considered themselves misogynistic. They had nothing against women in the same way that they had nothing against cattle or dogs. They understood that the function of a woman was to maintain the house, either as mistress of the premises or as a slave or servant working for its upkeep. A woman had the further task of birthing the next generation, in which female children had value as future brides to be bartered off for the best return politically or financially.

When a city was conquered in war it was considered straightforward enough that the conquerors killed the men and enslaved the women. In the *Odyssey* (bk 9) the heroic Odysseus remarks matter-of-factly, 'The wind took me first to Ismarus, which is the city of the Cicons. There I sacked the town and put the people to the sword. We took their wives for sex, domestic service, and loot.' In the *Iliad*, when Achilles organizes funeral games for his slain friend Patroclus, the prizes for the winners in each event include bronze tripods, women and horses.

It is also noteworthy that while many translations of Homer refer to 'wives' or 'concubines', in the original Greek the characters tend to use an all-purpose term meaning something like 'bed-mate'. Insofar as love entered into these relationships, it was felt by the female and seldom reciprocated. Women were silly, weak, lustful and capricious rather than suitable soul-mates.

Again, when the Greeks went to war with the Trojans over the abduction of Helen, it mattered not that Helen went willingly. Paris took her when he should not have done, so this was 'abduction'. After the war was over and Paris had been killed and Troy destroyed, Helen was taken back to Sparta where she resumed her duties as a royal spouse. In Homer no-one contemplated punishing Helen for the same reason that no-one punishes a horse that wanders out of the pasture if the gate is unlocked. What would be the point? (Later Greek playwrights such as Euripides felt that Helen *should* have been punished somehow, thus reflecting the growing suspicion in his day that women might actually be responsible for their own actions.)

Also the 21st century perception of women in myth shows the change in the status of victims between the ancient and modern eras. In the ancient world women as victims – and women not called Medea very often were victims – did not receive the sympathy and support to which we now feel they should be entitled. In the ancient viewpoint a victim was either unlucky (and therefore to be shunned), weak or incompetent (therefore ditto) or hated by the gods (ditto, with extra dits). Even female victims felt the same way – in stories told by male narrators.

Consider Briseus, of the generation after Medea. Her city of Lyrnessus was attacked by Achilles and his warriors. Achilles personally killed her parents and brothers and then expected her to serve without resentment as his concubine – which apparently she did (or at least Achilles had no complaints). In fact her main ambition, according to Homer, was to get promoted from concubine to the legal wife of Achilles. As a victim of abduction and rape, Briseus had no status and this fact - rather than resentment against the killer of her family seems to have motivated her the most.

The idea that women could directly intervene in politics in such a world was unthinkable. Women were not players, they were pieces. Like Briseus they were to be taken, traded and used to better the position of those in power over them. (Briseus ended up being given to a comrade of Achilles along with his armour and other personal effects.) Of course some women did get involved in politics anyway – royal women were not prepared to sit idly by and let mutton-headed menfolk decide the fate of their children. But there were acceptable ways to do this - a woman with strong opinions on a matter would seek out the man best able to influence events and attempt to sway him by using her feminine wiles.

Athenian women depicted on a black-figure vase collect water for the household.

Thus, during the Trojan war Zeus was frequently draped with female divinities whispering soft nothings into his ear as they tried to influence the fate of the Greeks, the Trojans or one favourite mortal or the other. Hera, queen of the gods demonstrates in the *Iliad* (2.14.155ff) how female influence should be used. At the time Hera wanted Zeus distracted so that she could aid the Greeks - although her lord and master had ordered her to stay out of the fight.

Now Hera of the golden throne ... saw Zeus, hateful to her heart, seated on the topmost peak of Mt Ida of the many springs. Then ox-eyed, queenly Hera pondered how she might deceive the mind of Zeus .... And this plan seemed best to her. She would go to Mount Ida, beautifully adorned, so he would want to lie by her side and embrace her body in love.

[There follows over a hundred lines detailing Hera's toilette, clothing and jewellery - Homer had a female audience also.]

Zeus, the cloud-gatherer beheld her and his heart was filled with lust. The son of Cronus clasped his wife in his arms ... and the two lay there swathed in a golden cloud from which fell drops of sparkling dew. And soon the father of the gods fell asleep, conquered by love in the arms of his wife.

Sleep was what Hera intended all along. Indeed she had arranged with Somnos, the god of sleep to sedate Zeus directly after her lovemaking. This she had done with a bribe, showing that women were also capable of buying into the prevailing sentiment of the times. She had vowed to Somnos that in exchange for his services, 'I will give you one of the Graces to make your wife. How about Pasithea, after whom you have always lusted?' Once Zeus was safely slumbering, Hera was able to aid her Greek heroes in inflicting great damage upon the Trojans.

From the point of view of Medea's contemporaries this was how a woman, if she had to do politics at all, should go about it. Persuasion, guile, behind-the-scenes manipulation of powerful males, all this was fair play. But to actually bypass a male agent and do one's killing personally – that was totally unsuitable for a woman. Why, it suggested that women could actually get things done in palace politics without male involvement, which was not only unthinkable but downright insulting.

Added to this was outrage at the creative sadism which Medea had displayed in perpetrating her crime. She had made the king's loving daughters first stab him and then chop up his corpse and then stand waiting as hope and expectation changed slowly to guilt and horror. Pelias had died believing that his daughters had betrayed him and wanted to kill him. The daughters lived with the shame that they had been agents in their own father's murder and in the very messy desecration of his corpse.

This is not how it should have been done. As a woman Medea should have gone to Jason, begged him to take his throne by force and so secure her future and that of their future children. Then Jason should have gathered as many heroes as were still available from the *Argo*, marched on the palace and slain Pelias by the sword. Instead he had been sent abroad to give himself an alibi while his wife did the dirty work – and to add insult to extreme injury – his wife had done it superbly.

Secondly, Medea was a foreigner. For the people of Iolcus the obvious reason why Medea had acted barbarously was precisely because she was a barbarian. At this time there was no such thing as a Greek – the term would be invented by the Romans almost half a millennium later. Even 'Hellene' was not a common term – the people of the time referred to themselves as Danaans, Achaeans or occasionally Argives. Nevertheless, for all that they lived in separate cities and kingdoms, the people of the peninsula shared a language and a common culture of which they were inordinately proud. Thales was grateful for being a Greek and not a barbarian because he and his contemporaries considered it indisputable that they were the finest specimens of humanity to walk the earth.

There was no doubt in the minds of the people of Iolcus that Jason had done Medea a huge favour in letting her 'assist' him in obtaining the Golden Fleece, because as a result (to quote Jason himself later) 'I took you from a barbarous house and a barbarous land and brought you to a Greek one'. While the word 'Greek' here is anachronistic, the sentiment that Euripides has Jason express is that which any countryman of his time would have felt.

True, the Egyptians had a civilization thousands of years older, and across the Aegean Sea there were peoples whose achievements in art, architecture and almost every other form of cultural expression far outshone anything the Greeks had yet achieved, but all of this could be discounted because such peoples were 'barbarian'. Those benighted savages had no real recognition of how a man should live his life, worship the gods or do business with others. In later years the Greeks would have very good reason to feel themselves culturally superior to other nations (though these reasons were never quite as good as the Greeks felt them to be), but in fact the feeling came before the achievements.

Medea was a princess, yes, but a princess of Colchis – a nation infamous for its wild, hostile landscape, its poisonous flora and savage people. She was the granddaughter of a god, certainly, but nevertheless - she was an outsider. That stark fact meant that in some ways Medea had lower standing than a pure-bred Hellenic servant girl. It did not help that the Greeks then and later favoured blonde hair and pale complexions. (Some Greek women wore hats with a brim only, so that their faces could be shaded while their hair was bleached blonde.) Yet Herodotus, writing in the fifth century BC, takes pains to tell us that the average Colchian had a particularly swarthy complexion. So much so that he felt that their appearance gave credibility to the idea that the original Colchians had been Egyptian.

So we have the dark-complexioned Medea, a strange woman from a barbarous land who had terrifying magical powers over life and death - but also no idea how a civilized person should behave. Instead of showing gratitude at being accepted into superior Greek culture and being properly submissive while she learned how to conduct herself, she had promptly and effortlessly exterminated the local king. And she had done this in a manner that contrived to make the king's death a humiliating disgrace and his daughters (pure-bred Hellenic royalty who had condescended to befriend her!) into credulous dupes.

Medea had overlooked a third alternative by which the daughters of Pelias could try to escape punishment for their actions. She had foreseen that could have covered up their crime and made their father inexplicably vanish, or that they could claim they they were staging a palace coup. She had not anticipated a defence that 'the foreign witch made us do it'. Yet once that claim was made it is unsurprising that local uneasiness about Medea rapidly escalated into a storm of outrage in which fear, sexism and xenophobia all played an equal part.

While Jason had not been involved in the murder, this did not really help his case. He was Medea's husband and therefore he should have known what his woman was up to. As a Greek male it was his job to keep Medea under control – something he had signally failed to do. And if the man could not even manage his own household, how was he supposed to run the kingdom?

It did not help that there was another excellent candidate for king waiting in the wings. This was Acastus, the son of the deceased and dismembered Pelias. Acastus had been away the past few years so he was not associated with the more homicidal aspects of his father's later rule. Furthermore, the reason that he had been away was because he was a member of the crew of the *Argo* while they retrieved the Golden Fleece, so Acastus had already demonstrated that he had the heroic chops required for a Heroic Age king.

That is, even though he was the son of the King, Acastus was not a 'prince', because that is not how kingship worked in contemporary Greece. Homer frequently refers to kings as 'ruling by might'. By this he does not mean that the king is a tyrant, but only that in the rough times in which his characters lived, one did not remain a king unless one could hold on to the job - by force if need be. Acastus was not a 'prince' because this implies a hereditary right to the throne which did not exist in Medea's Greece. It was certainly true that a king through the power of his connections, the strength of his household and the extent of his family lands could leave a son well-placed to take over

Funeral scene and chariot from the early archaic era when the Medea legend was first written down.

his position. However if the other noblemen of the state felt strongly enough about it, the only position which the son might attain would be in a grave beside his father's.

Adroitly, Acastus first demonstrated his filial piety and the wealth of his household by holding magnificent funeral games for his father. (The heroine Atalanta makes a brief cameo reappearance here, defeating Peleus in a wrestling match which was part of the games.) Then while he populace and aristocrats were still awed by the splendour of the games, Acastus declared himself king and promptly booted his rival Jason and his disturbing wife Medea into exile. He also exiled his sisters for their part in his father's death. What thereafter became of those unfortunate women is unknown.

The exile of Medea was a very popular move with the people of Iolcus and built upon Acastus' already good start. It also established what was to be something of an ongoing tradition for Medea, whereby when she left town she did so in a hurry, often with armed pursuit not far behind.

It is also interesting that Medea's sojourns in different places each mark a different stage in the life of a typical Greek woman. In Colchis she had been an unmarried maiden (*kore*), while in Iolcus she was a married but childless woman (*nymphe*). Doubtless Medea hoped that while in exile she would transition to a wife and mother (*gyne*). This was the final stage which marked a complete and full life for a Hellenic woman. It is doubtful though, that this marked the limit of Medea's ambitions.

Fortunately for the new exiles, the leadership of

Greece was something of a family affair. While today we tend to think of Greece as the world's first democracy, this form of government lay half a millennium in the future of Athens and it never really caught on elsewhere in Greece. In Medea's day the land was divided into dozens of statelets, many as small as Iolcus, all of which were ruled by kings. At this time the gods took an active interest in the affairs of humanity, and many of these affairs were, well, affairs. Greek gods paid little attention to the marital status of those whom they intended to seduce (or rape – Greek gods were not very clear about the difference). As a result most of the kingdoms of Heroic Age Greece had rulers who were linked by ties of dynastic marriage or because someone in the family line had impregnated or been impregnated by the same god. (Zeus at one time managed to become his own great-uncle by marriage.)

As a result of this nexus of family connections Jason and Medea were able to find refuge in Corinth where both had relatives, Jason through an ancestor called Creusus, and Medea through Sisyphus. In fact, in one version of the Medea story the Corinthians asked for Medea to come to them - 'Corinthus, the son of Marathon, died without an heir so the Corinthians sent to Medea in Iolcus ... and thus through her Jason received the kingdom.' (Pausanias 2.3.10 -11)

In other words, when Jason and Medea arrived in Corinth they did not do so as penniless refugees but as welcome guests who were immediately plugged into the top echelon of Corinthian society.

It is probable that Medea had pondered the lesson of why she had been expelled from Iolcus, and she was determined to not make the same mistake in Corinth. Here she would be an impeccable Greek wife, outwardly deferential to her husband and learning to be more Greek than the Greeks in her speech and conduct. This dealt with, or at least papered over the 'woman' and 'barbarian' character defects which the Greek world assigned to her. More problematic was the issue of magic - but this was not a problem in the same way, and not the reason that Medea had been exiled from Iolcus.

Medea is generally considered a witch, yet the ancient writers go to some lengths not to ascribe supernatural powers to her. For example, while raising Aeson from the dead in Iolcus, Medea did not merely wave a magic wand and chant hocus-pocus. She had to travel the length and breadth of Greece gathering specific herbs, plants and animal material and she achieved her results through knowing the correct procedures. Likewise, while preparing Jason for his trials in Colchis, Medea had to use specific unguents rather than simply bestowing invulnerability upon him.

When Medea did work magic, as she did in blinding Talos, the bronze man of Crete, this was done by invoking powers from the Underworld to do her bidding. The implication of this is that Medea was not herself a particularly supernatural being, but was a particularly adept student and user of supernatural materials. (And we shall examine in a moment why even the term 'supernatural' is not particularly useful in this discussion.)

Medea's main advantage lay not in her magical powers but in her connection with superhuman forces. While anyone with the time and application might gather many of the materials in Medea's pharmacopoeia, not many people would have the sort of personal relationship with Hecate whereby the goddess could explain the power and preparation of each herb. Nor could most people ask their grandfather for a personal dragon-drawn chariot that could whip them around the known world in the blink of an eye.

Given the promiscuous nature of the Greek gods there were many people in the land of Hellas who shared Medea's divine relations, yet very few of them went on to become successful magic users. Indeed, magic and spells play a relatively small part in Greek myth and none in major events like the Trojan War. What made Medea successful at magic was her intense dedication to her studies, her innate ability to see possible solutions where others only saw problems, and a psychopathic disregard for collateral damage when it came to turning those possible solutions into reality. These were qualities that did not in themselves mark Medea as an outsider in the same way as did her gender and Colchian origins.

This is also because in the world of heroic Greece practically everything counted as 'magic'. Medea was a master of magic because magic was everywhere - if only one knew how to use it. Her world knew nothing of electron imbalances and colliding air masses but was very familiar with lightning and thunder, and everyone knew that only great power could generate such phenomena. Was it so hard to believe in returning from the dead or magical transformations in a world where flowers became fruit, trees returned to life every springtime and caterpillars turned into cocoons then butterflies?

Centaurs, demons and other 'supernatural' species are not in themselves inherently less credible than hippopotami, crocodiles and gorillas – all species with which the Greeks were vaguely acquainted. The Roman writer Pliny advised women to take pellets of hare dung to avoid developing saggy breasts, yet the ancient sceptic who mocked such treatments would probably also be incredulous that chewing willow bark might avert the symptoms of rheumatism. (Which it does – the original chemicals for aspirin were extracted from willow bark.)

In the modern world we use the scientific method to establish what is possible and what is not, and agree that the only way that the latter might be achieved is through magic. (Then we go on to achieve through science what previous generations would have called magic anyway, but that is not the point.) The point is that Medea's magic was credible and acceptable because it was achieved through study, hard work and personal connections, and because in her day it was simply not known what was scientifically possible and what was not.

She lived in a world packed with phenomena that no-one could explain even though they encountered them on a daily basis. Medea had made herself expert at manipulating and exploiting those phenomena, but this was a personal achievement, not an inherent property as was being female and non-Greek. In a world which respected achievement, this made her magic almost acceptable in away that barbaric womanhood was not.

Thus, after her first bruising encounter with the Greek world in Iolcus, Medea had learned how she could make that world accept, or at least tolerate, her in Corinth. She could cover, or at least compensate for her own perceived flaws. Nevertheless she was still stuck with an irredeemably flawed husband.

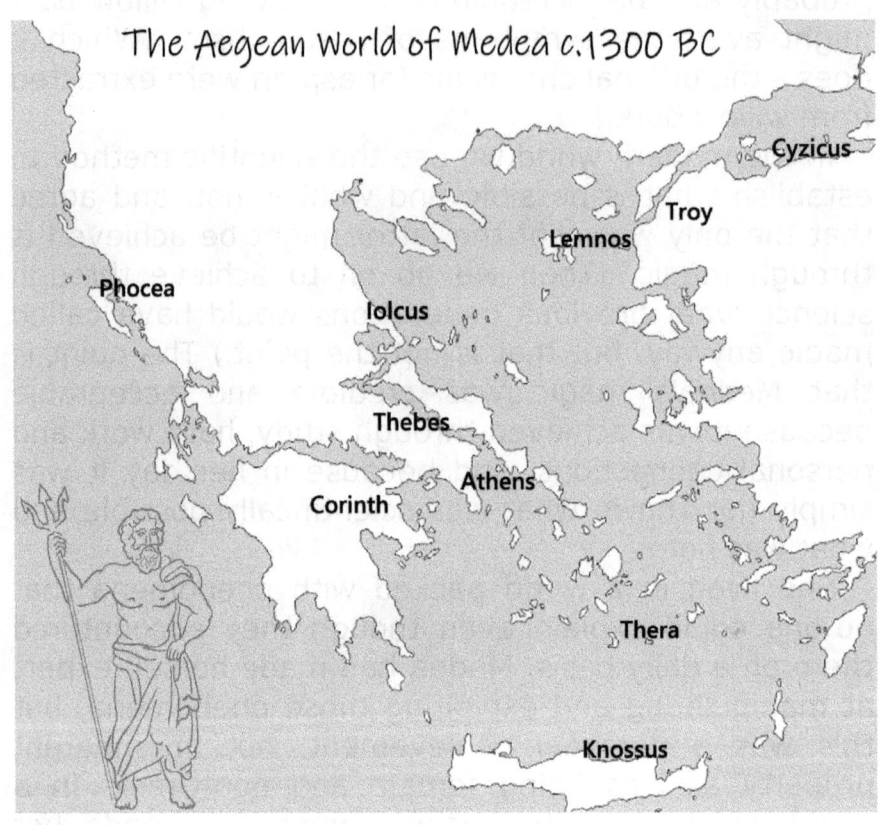

Chapter 9

Irreconcilable Differences

At some point during the early years of Medea's stay in Corinth she was treated to a demonstration as to how one was meant to go about overthrowing a heroic age king according to the proper conventions that she had so brutally violated. The about-to-be-former king of Iolcus in question was Acastus, son of Pelias

After the expulsion of Medea and Jason, the little kingdom was looking forward to a spell of peace and quiet after the recent dynastic turmoil. The fearsome Medea was now living quietly in Corinth with Jason, the only other credible contender for the throne. The troublesome heroes from the *Argo* had largely dispersed to their homes, though one of them, Peleus, had remained.

Peleus and Acastus had a relationship pre-dating the voyage of the *Argo*, because Acastus had once purified Peleus for the accidentally-on-purpose slaying of a rival during the famous hunt for the Calydonian Boar. Peleus was in no hurry to return to his home on the isle of Aegina (near Athens). He took part in the funeral games which Acastus staged for his father and on this occasion was comprehensively beaten in a wrestling competition. His opponent was the formidable Atalanta, who thus gained some revenge for being omitted from the crew of the *Argo* on account of her gender.

IRRECONCILABLE DIFFERENCES

Now Peleus whiled away time at the royal palace, drinking and yarning with his royal companion.

The hero Atalanta, from a mosaic now in the British Museum

This brought Peleus into frequent contact with the wife of Acastus, one Astydameia (though some sources call her Hippolyte). It turned out that this contact was neither as frequent nor as intimate as Astydameia wished and she made this very plain to Peleus. The hero vehemently rejected the advances of Astydameia, perhaps because of personal integrity – her husband was his close friend after all – but more probably because he was engaged to marry the nymph, Thetis.

Thetis had contacts that went all the way to the very top and was a personal favourite of Zeus himself. In fact, Thetis was friend to most of the Olympian gods - all of whom were already invited to her planned nuptials - and step-mother to one of these gods. (Hephaestus, the Craftsman God).

Peleus was not going to risk a well-aimed thunderbolt by stepping out on his betrothed with a woman to whom he was not even particularly attracted and he informed Astydameia of the fact in no uncertain terms. Astydameia did not take rejection well.

Thetis and Peleus were not already married because Peleus already had a wife back in Aegina. The gods knew that this unfortunate woman was already doomed. If Peleus shared this knowledge, he was not going to add to her misfortunes by committing adultery.

Yet it turned out that his very abstinence caused his wife's death because the rejected Astydameia vindictively wrote a letter to the lady, gloatingly informing her that Peleus was staying on in Iolcus because he was going to get a divorce and thereafter marry a daughter of Acastus. On hearing the false news, the devastated wife hanged herself – as the gods had already known she would.

Yet Astydameia was not yet done. She next went to her husband Acastus and informed him that Peleus had raped her. Acastus believed the accusation but bided his time in plotting revenge. (He was the son of scheming Pelias, after all.) A few days after the fateful accusation, Acastus cheerfully announced that it was time to go hunting on a nearby mountain. The game was abundant there because no ordinary hunter dared go near the place, which was infested with centaurs who had a strong dislike of humanity. Nevertheless, even the centaurs would be wary of taking on a pair of well-armed heroes so Peleus probably imagined that the expedition was safe enough.

Of course, Peleus did not reckon on the fact that Acastus would silently abandon him in the night and ride off with his weapons, horse and armour, leaving him defenceless and alone in a very hostile environment. This abandonment was not merely creative sadism (though this probably factored in also) but because Acastus was well aware that Thetis would take a dim view of the killing of her intended spouse. Better then, to have the actual deed done by someone else.

Acastus had underestimated how closely the gods were following the activities of Peleus. Nasty and xenophobic the centaurs certainly were but even they changed their views about the visitor abandoned on their mountain after a visit from the very persuasive Hermes. Once made keenly aware of the consequences of harming a single hair on the head of Peleus, the centaurs spared no effort in seeing him swiftly escorted to safety.

Along the way someone brought Peleus up to speed with what had been going on. The furious Peleus was not without contacts of his own and he quickly mustered an army largely consisting of the former crewmen of the *Argo*, their allies and retainers. Included in this group was Jason, who had a bone or two of his own to pick with Acastus. Little Iolcus (present-day population 2,146) was speedily overwhelmed by the superior force.

Acastus perished, though it is uncertain whether in battle or after his defeat. His treacherous wife Astydameia finally got her wish of having Peleus between her legs because Peleus had her split in two before he and his entire army marched triumphantly between the gory remains. (There is a possible link here with the ancient vernal tradition of the *Xanthika* in northern Greece where the army was marched between the separated halves of a slain dog. If Peleus had this tradition in mind he was definitely adding insult to lethal injury.)

Since Peleus had no further interest in Iolcus it fell to Jason to arrange the subsequent management of the place. The kingdom still wanted nothing to do with him or Medea but a child of his royal line was acceptable. This led to the first-born of Jason and Medea being moved out of the blast radius of his parents' increasingly dysfunctional marriage and later installed as king of Iolcus. Indeed, it seems that the entire region of Thessaly was later named after this king - who bore the name of Thessalus.

A minor footnote to the Medea legend is inserted at this point by one Antiochus. Antiochus was author of a work called the *Legends of Iolcus* and he evidently had something against Cretans. Though his work is lost, the relevant part still exists in summary. It seems that Jason and Medea were visiting Iolcus when they met Peleus and his now-wife Thetis on a similar trip.

While in Thessalia, Thetis and Medea disagreed as to whom was the more beautiful. As judge they chose Idomeneus [then the king of Crete, whose reasons for being in Iolcus are unknown] *He gave the prize to Thetis.*

The angered Medea exclaimed that the Cretans were liars and in revenge she cursed them that they always would be liars, just as their king had lied in his judgement. This is why Cretans are now considered incapable of telling the truth.

Photius, *Myriobiblon* 190

This incidentally gives us an unusual insight as to how Medea's myth has been passed through the generations, for the ancient academics who tell this story take the unusual step of quoting their sources. So we know that Antiochus was cited by one Athenodoros of Eretria, in Book Eight of his *Commentaries*. Athenodoros was then cited by Ptolemy Hephaestion in Book Five of his *New History* and the final result cited here is from the only one of these texts to have survived from antiquity – Hephaestion, quoted in the works of Photius, a Byzantine scholar of the ninth century.

Back in Corinth, Medea was on a slow burn. She was trying very hard to be good, but Jason and the Corinthians were not making it easy. Given Jason's standing, Medea mixed regularly with the cream of Corinthian society who made veiled sneers at her conduct whenever she acted in a non-Corinthian (let alone non-Greek) manner. Medea did her best to fit in, remarking to the Corinthian ladies, 'Above all a stranger should adopt a city's views. I don't approve of anyone who has a heart so stubborn as to oafishly resent the city's will' (Euripides *Medea* l.222). Yet even when Medea acted impeccably she was rewarded with patronizing praise at how well she had assimilated 'for a barbarian'.

Jason himself was of a similar opinion, telling her, 'You have received from me more than you ever gave. Now you live in Greece, instead of a barbarian land. You have learned what justice means, and how people live by the law.' (ibid I.640)

Jason not only felt that he had done Medea a favour by taking her from her homeland to Greece, he made it plain that he was suffering for it – daily he had to endure condescension for sullying himself by taking a barbarian wife. Nor was he above explaining to Medea what embarrassment his marriage was causing him. As Medea herself remarked, her marriage was doomed once 'your foreign wife became a shame to you' (ibid I.753).

Medea bore all this in silence for almost a decade. Privately she referred to the Corinthians as the 'race of Sisyphus' (infamous for murder, incest, necrophilia and betraying the trust of Zeus himself). Yet on account of her marriage to Jason she was the 'laughing stock of this breed; she who was the grand-daughter of the sun-god Helios' (ibid I.483), whose aunts were queen Pasiphae of Crete, Circe the sorceress and Selene, goddess of the Moon.

Medea had not become the foremost magical practitioner of her generation without considerable training in patience and self-control. Nevertheless, a decade is a long time in which to suffer in silence, especially since Medea being Medea, every hurt and slight was ignored but never forgotten. One way or another an explosion was coming.

That explosion has been documented by a number of writers and in later ages has been the subject of books, plays and psychological studies. Our principal sources are the playwright Euripides and Seneca (the tutor and mentor of the young Roman Emperor Nero) who wrote texts about it. The poet Ovid provides further details in his usual sensationalist style and various other ancient authors have chipped in. Not all of these versions agree on a single story-line and, in fact, some are downright contradictory. Yet from the mixture it is possible to synthesize a single version of events and it is this which is given below (with acknowledgements where individual writers veer from the canon).

It was Jason who precipitated the disaster that was to change Medea's life and ruin his own. Over the years he had become increasingly friendly with Creon, the king of Corinth. One day Jason came home to announce marvellous news. He had managed to secure an excellent future for their children! They would henceforth be brought up alongside the children of the royal household. To secure this wonderful outcome all that Jason had to do was divorce Medea and marry Creusa, the King's daughter. Regrettably, for some reason the King felt that Medea might have hard feelings about this great opportunity. Therefore, she was ordered to get out of Corinth immediately. Did she need any help with packing her things?

Medea's outraged response was met with Jason's bland and deliberate incomprehension to that outrage. According to his self-serving reasoning ...

Look, I left Iolcus with apparently insoluble problems following me. So how much better could it work out than that I, an exile, should marry the daughter of a king? I'm not doing this because you are loathsome to me – perish the thought – and not because I really want a new bride. Nor do I necessarily want more children, Those I have are sufficient, so no complaints about your performance on that score.

No, I'm doing this so that we – and this is very important – we can live in comfort without fear of destitution. No-one is friends with a pauper. Here's an opportunity to raise my sons as befits children of a royal house. I'll be father to new brothers for the children you have borne me and all shall be raised to a new high rank. Thus, my present family benefits from the family that is yet to be.

So, what have I done wrong? Even you would say I have not if your heart was not poisoned by envy for another woman. Really, you women have such strange ideas. You think all is well in the world as long as your married life runs smoothly. But if some misfortune disturbs your love, suddenly you hate everything that you considered good and lovely before.

Euripides Medea l.650ff

The best one could say for Jason is that he was consistent. Every time he thought it best for himself, he was prepared not only to throw Medea to the wolves but to try first to persuade her that he was doing so in her best interest – a fault of which Medea was well aware. 'He's so sure that his tongue can hide injustice that he'll dare to do anything' (ibid, l.692).

Steal the Fleece for him and so betray father and country? Oh definitely, because that way we can be happy together. About to be caught by the pursuing Colchians? Well, let me hand you over to them my dear, so that way we can both survive. (Well, you probably, I certainly - and I'll still have the Fleece.) Abandon you for the King's daughter? Yes! Think of the children and don't be ungrateful for the opportunity I have found for them. 'Show more wisdom', quoth he, 'and never let happiness be disguised as sorrow, or

when fortune smiles on you, don't pretend she frowns.'

When Medea began recounting the sacrifices she had made for Jason and the crimes she had committed for his success, Jason brushed these aside. Great as these blessings had been, Medea had been driven by love - and for that Cypris [Aphrodite] was responsible. If Jason owed anyone thanks it was to the goddess, the instigator of Medea's actions, rather than to Medea herself - the tool by which Aphrodite had accomplished her purpose.

Jason and Medea: Part of a 1759 painting by Charles-Andre van Loo

Then Jason tried to put a positive spin even upon Medea's forthcoming exile. Medea had travelled with the

Argonauts, he pointed out, and these were among the leading citizens in their own lands. If Medea were armed with a commendation from Jason, surely one of these men would find a home for her. There she could remain in comfort, warmed by the glowing thought that back in Corinth her children were being raised as princes. Jason himself, once settled comfortably in the palace, would try to find out where Medea had eventually settled and make sure that she was comfortably off, even if he had to pay for it himself. Could anyone say fairer than that?

It is possible that Jason was trying to convince himself that he was guiltless, because he was certainly not convincing Medea. The only reason that the pair had got as far as Corinth was because Medea was certainly not stupid. That Jason was now treating her as if she were indeed an idiot only added to her fury and anguish.

Bitterly she pointed out that there could be no return to Colchis for her and Iolcus was out of the question. As an exile cast off by her husband, she was vulnerable to those from Iolcus, Crete, and Colchis who had good reason to wish her ill. If Jason himself had discarded her, which of the heroes of the *Argo* would be prepared to take in such uncomfortable guest with such dangerous potential enemies?

In Euripides, the chorus asks Medea (ibid l.350) 'Where will you turn? Where will you find someone to take you in? What country, what home will you find to save you from misfortune?' One is reminded of the epic scene in *Gone with the Wind* where Scarlett O'Hara cries 'Where shall I go, what shall I do?'

This time, however, it is Jason whose response amo-

IRRECONCILABLE DIFFERENCES

unts to 'Frankly Medea, I don't give a damn.'

And on that note Jason went off to prepare for his forthcoming nuptials, leaving his wife desolate. In Euripides, the couple's nurse describes Medea in the aftermath of the devastating meeting.

Disgraced, that poor lady sobs, repeating his promises, the trust that she placed in that right hand with which he pledged his love. She calls on the gods to witness how Jason has repaid all that she has done for him.

She won't eat - her body is wasting away. She just lies there, giving herself up to her pain. She has ever been in tears since she discovered how her husband has dishonoured her. She keeps her gaze fixed on the ground and listens to the words of well-wishers, or even her friends as though she were a statue ... . Now and then she turns her white neck as she weeps for her father, her home and her native land – all things she abandoned for the man who has now abandoned her.

Euripides *Medea* ll 20-45

Desolate and heartbroken Medea might be, but the nurse knew her mistress. Later, she concludes prophetically.

Anyone can see that the bitter grief steaming off her is just the start. Her mood is getting more intense and her temper will soon catch fire. The passion in that soul is hard to contain. What will she do next, now her heart has been stung by these hurts? ... She's a dangerous woman.

Things won't be easy for any man who picks a fight with her,

even when he thinks she's beaten and he's triumphed.
(ll 129-134)

Euripides now sends the chorus, a troop of Corinthian ladies who have come to see for themselves how the marital drama will play out. The leader asks with sympathy (feigned or otherwise)

Aristocratic Corinthian woman in a painting from the time of Euripides

I've heard her voice, the cries of that sad lady here from Colchis. One of the household servants told me that she's been screaming. Has she not calmed down yet? Nurse, this house's suffering brings me no pleasure. We've been friends, you know. (l. 157 ff)

IRRECONCILABLE DIFFERENCES

Medea leaves the house to confront this delegation and at this point delivers a speech as heartfelt as it is deceptively ingenuous, demonstrating that it is not only Jason who can present alternative facts as reality. These oft-quoted words are among the most famous in all the works of Euripides and are worth giving in their entirety not only because of what Medea has to say but also because of the hard truths about contemporary marriage that the playwright unloads upon the menfolk of Athens. (ibid l. 213ff)

Women of Corinth, I'm coming out of my house so you won't think badly of me. It's easy to get a reputation for being aloof or arrogant because someone stays in the comfort of their home.

Medea now gets in a quick dig at how she has been received in Corinth

There's no justice in the eyes of mortals – even before they really get to know what someone is like and without receiving any hurt from her, they hate her on sight ... my joy in life has been destroyed by unexpected misfortune. I simply want to die.

From here Medea tries to recruit the women as allies by a technique as old as marriage – complaining about her husband. At the same time Euripides, through Medea, points out how inequitable marriage actually was in the Athens of his day.

My own husband, he who was everything to me, has turned out to be the worst of men. So now, this I have found to be true. Of all beings

that have life and awareness, none are more unfortunate than women. First, we need a husband, though what we get is not worth what we pay. To add to our misfortune and our grief, he is then master of our bodies, even before we've got to grips with the crucial question - this man we're stuck with, is he good or bad? Yet we can't refuse to have a husband and getting a divorce loses a woman all respect

She goes into her husband's home with its new rules and different customs. Then she needs a prophet's talent to figure out the nature of the man who shares her bed. You don't learn that at your childhood home. We work hard at this, and if we succeed, the husband accepts being yoked in marriage and we live in peace – that's a life to envy. But fail, and death is by far the better option. If a man gets tired of your company at home he goes and finds relief elsewhere – perhaps a male friend or someone his own age. [Athenian brides tended to be around fifteen years younger than their husbands.] *We women are stuck with that one man.*

According to our menfolk we stay safe and secure at home while they carry their spears into battle. The idiots. I would rather stand three times with a shield in the battle-line than once give birth.

At this point Medea veers off to take a very lop-sided look at her own case.

But your story and mine are not the same. For you have a city, and the houses of your fathers. You have friends and company and an enjoyable life. Personally, I have no city and no refuge from an abusive husband [Though Jason was never accused of actually being abusive]. *He carried me off as a trophy from a barbarian*

IRRECONCILABLE DIFFERENCES

country. [Though Medea was not actually kidnapped.] *Now I have no mother, brother or family member to shelter me in my distress.* [Which is reminiscent of the man who murdered his parents and then asked the court for mercy because he was an orphan.]

Now here's what I ask of you. Say nothing if I work out how to punish Jason. Or punish his bride. Or her father ... Look, if there's steel flashing in battle, then a woman can show timidity. But if her marriage is violated and she is wounded in love, no heart yearns more eagerly for blood.

One gets a chilling insight into the character of Medea when she later reveals to a friend how she plans 'to strike a mortal blow at Jason'. The appalled friend replies, 'But Medea, as a woman this act will destroy you.'

Medea replies, 'That is beside the point.'

Chapter 10

Preparations

Medea had little love for Creon, King of Corinth. It was he who had colluded with the treacherous Jason to tear apart her marriage and order a unilateral divorce. Any revenge that Medea took on Jason had to include the King. Seneca has her muttering -

It's all Creon's fault. No-one can stop him from dissolving marriages and tearing mothers from their children and he can break promises made by the strongest oaths. So, him also I shall attack. When he pays his debt, his home will be piled high with ashes – Malea [the furthest point in southern Greece] *will see the flames leaping from the dark gables of his palace.*

Seneca Medea 1.137

Creon was well aware of the threat posed by Medea. Indeed, he had been all for having her executed before she was even aware that Jason planned a divorce, but Jason's pleas had swayed him. Creon still (rightly) considered that Medea was a lethal threat but he did not want his relationship with his new son-in-law to start on a bad footing. Therefore, Creon had agreed that Medea would be spared, but only on condition that she left Corinth – immediately. Yet it seemed that she was still on the premises and, indeed, had just spoken with her ex-husband-to-be.

PREPARATIONS

That baleful child of Colchian Aeëtes, Medea, is still in my realm? She is cunning and powerful – and she's up to something. The only question is whom she will spare to live in peace. It would have been so expedient to be rid of this ghastly threat with the sword. But no, I had to listen to the prayers of her husband. Well, she's been given her life but she has to leave my lands and free them from fear.
(Ibid l.179)

The lofty Acrocorinth. Creon's palace, first destroyed by Medea, and further dilapidated in later eras.

Creon then stormed out of the palace to give Medea her notice of eviction in person. On his arrival Medea pitched her case – not against the divorce but against the decree of exile.

168

Creon, let me ask you something. Since I'm the victim here, why banish me? What have I done to you? Have I hurt you? Made you suffer? Yes, I've done terrible things, but none through malice. My motive was always love for Jason. It was for him that Pelias died, not for me. Yes, you can add theft, elopement and a mutilated brother – all crimes that Jason is probably teaching his new bride. I've been guilty, but never for myself. I should be considered guiltless in the sight of he for whom I was guilty.
(Ibid. l.272ff)

Medea also points out what no-one wanted to acknowledge – without her aid the Argonauts would have perished several times over.

This alone is what I brought with me from Colchis the salvation of the flower of Hellas. ... Orpheus is my gift; he whose singing can soften stone and draw down the trees. My gift to Greece is also the lives of the twins, Castor and Pollux ... the sons of Boreas, and Lynceus, and...'.
(ibid l.223ff)

Creon's reply was blunt.

'I'll be honest - you scare me. And I know well you're capable of killing my daughter. The way I see it, you're a clever woman experienced in harm ejected from her husband's bed. And I hear you've been making threats ... so, I'm taking precautions. Enduring your hatred is preferable to later regret for being compassionate now.'
Euripides Medea l.283ff

PREPARATIONS

Creon then added another twist. 'You must go into exile and take those children of yours with you.'

Taken aback, Medea asks. 'My children? Are they also to be blamed for my guilt?'

It should be remembered that Jason originally tried to persuade Medea that he was marrying Creon's daughter purely for the benefit of their children. Once he had remarried, they were to be raised with the royal household.

Seneca in his *Medea* sticks to this line, but in the Euripides version Creon shows it to be a blatant lie. Jason only wanted to be shot of his inconvenient wife but Creon wanted to be rid also of Jason's equally inconvenient children. So much for Jason's promise.

I want to raise my children properly, as befits my rank. There will be brothers to the children born from you, and I'll make them all the same. That way our united family [except you] will thrive.
(Ibid 1.594)

It may have been difficult for Jason to give Medea a lower opinion of himself than she already had but this further betrayal effortlessly achieved it. Thinking fast, Medea pointed out that if she had to make arrangements for her children also, she needed more time. An extra day at least. This was not an unreasonable request and it put Creon in something of a bind. It was clear that Medea was very much the wronged party here and as Creon frankly admitted, she was being exiled not for anything that she had done but through his fear of what she might do.

Could he, a king who like any contemporary monarch ruled through force of personality, admit that he was so afraid of one unarmed woman that he could not grant her one more day to ensure the welfare of her children? He had an army, a palace filled with armed retainers and a kingdom of loyal subjects. She was just one woman – even if that woman was Medea. How weak would he seem if he showed himself too timid to grant her even the small mercy of one more day before exile?

Therefore, he grudgingly conceded that one more day it would be. But if Medea was still within his borders come the following sunrise, he would have her hunted down and killed. Creon was well aware that Medea was probably planning something, but as Medea disingenuously enquired, what plan could she execute against someone with Creon's resources, and that in a single day? So, he declared

I'm too tender-hearted for a monarch and showing mercy has cost me before – more than once. So, though I can see I'm making a mistake, woman, you can have one more day. But know this, if sunrise tomorrow finds you within this country, I'll kill you – and your children. Please don't think this is a bluff. Stay if you must, but for a day. In that time, you can't be as dangerous as I fear.
(Ibid 347ff)

Medea then asked Creon to depart because the short time allowed before her forced departure left her with much to do. Creon accordingly took himself off, remarking pointedly that he had a wedding to arrange. He did not hear Medea murmur softly to his departing back, 'So then, you have not heard from Pelias?'

PREPARATIONS

Glauce/Cerusa, Jason's intended bride. (From the Medea Sarcophagus in Berlin)

Euripides in his play has Medea explain herself to the audience. (Our other main source, Seneca has a less introspective protagonist.) Musingly, Medea remarks,

Well, it looks bad – but that just means there's plenty of room for improvement. Newly-weds often face some difficulties, and the man who made this marriage happen may run into a few problems of his own. What? You think I'd demean myself by begging favours from a man like that if I didn't have an idea in mind? Now I have a whole day to turn the three of them into corpses – and there's so many ways of doing that I'm not sure which to try first.

This is a test of wills. I, the grand-daughter of Helios, am not going to end up the laughing-stock of Corinth. Once they're all dead, I need someone who can defend me, a city that will receive me when I ask for shelter. Otherwise I'll end it all with a sword. These people don't get to bring pain into my heart and then laugh about it.
(Ibid 354ff)

Accordingly, Medea set out to find Aegeus, the King of Athens whom she knew to be in town. Since no meeting was scheduled, Medea needed to bump into him 'accidentally'. As it happened, Aegeus may also have been looking to accidentally bump into Medea. King and exile each wanted something from the other.

Aegeus had just been to consult with the famed Oracle in Delphi. Despite his best efforts, the King was childless and wanted the Oracle to tell him what to do about it. While his trip to Delphi had not been as fruitless as his marriage, the King was uncertain what to make of the Oracle's cryptic response. Medea was pretty sure she could figure out what the Oracle was getting at, so she asked if it was permissible for Aegeus to share what he had been told. Aegeus was more than happy to do so.

'Do not untie the wineskin's out-jutting foot ...'

At which point Medea might have blinked at Aegeus with some surprise. The meaning of this statement was so clear that the Oracle's usually cryptic priestess must have been having a bad day. In those times, wine in Greece was usually stored in the whole skin of a young goat. Three of the legs were removed from the tanned hide, and the remaining leg served as a spigot for the container. To release the wine, you untied the knot at the end of the leg. Given that the question put to the Oracle related to childlessness, it was not hard to understand that the 'wineskin' in question held the royal testicles of Aegeus. As for the 'out-jutting foot' – well, was the man that naive? There had to be more.

Okay, reckoned Medea. Don't have sex. 'Until when? Until you do what or reach what destination?'

'Until I get back to Athens', the King explained. This answer immediately raised another question. Corinth does not lie on the route between Delphi and Athens and if the Oracle reckoned that it was in the King's best interest to get home, why the detour?

Aegeus explained that he was travelling to consult with his friend the King of Troezen who was reputed to be good at understanding such matters. This would ensure that there was no further insight to be gained from the oracle. Medea immediately knew that this was a bad idea. When a god tells you to keep it tucked under your tunic till you get home, you really don't want to extend your journey.

On the other hand, the nature of the prophetic warning (and Medea understood that this was a warning, not advice) told Medea not to get involved. Interfering with the inexorable workings of the Fates simply meant that one became part of the process by which the inevitable unfolded. Therefore, Medea carefully stepped back.

'Well, may good fortune help you find what you

want.' The oracle was not mentioned again – though Aegeus would have done well to take its advice.

Medea could however make the original purpose of the king's trip redundant. 'It's a stroke of luck that you ran into me. It's the Gods' answer to your desire to have children. With my potions you can have a swarm of them and die a happy man.'

There was one condition – those potions would have to be personally administered by Medea in Athens. In other words, Aegeus would have to take in the exiled Medea as a supplicant. Once Medea explained the circumstances which had caused her impending exile, Aegeus was shocked.

In marriage at that time a woman subordinated herself completely to her husband. In return the husband had a duty to care for his dependent wife. As Medea told Jason outright 'Unless you think the gods have changed how men should behave, you know you've broken your promises to me.' Aegeus' appalled reaction to Jason's conduct shows what a violation this was of contemporary standards of behaviour. This makes his reply all the more interesting.

Lady, I'm inclined to do you this favour. First for the Gods. And secondly for the children that you can have me produce. Here's the thing though. I'm a guest in Corinth and I won't have my hosts finding fault with me. If you reach Athens, I'll give you sanctuary.
You'll be safe there and I won't give you up to anyone. But you have to get there on your own – I'll not plot to help you escape from Corinth.

Euripides Medea l.719 passim

PREPARATIONS

Here's the thing. As matters stood at the time of this conversation there was no question of Medea having trouble leaving Corinth. She was the opposite of a prisoner. Creon wanted her out as soon as, and by any means, possible. If the King of Athens had proposed to take Medea away with him, Creon would probably have fallen on the man's neck in gratitude. So why 'plot' to achieve something when the people you're scheming against desperately want the same outcome? And ... 'escape'? Escape from what, exactly?

Part of the answer comes with Aegeus' words '... for the Gods'. Medea is the wronged party, and the gods of Greece were, above all, forces of order. Jason's - and Creon's - blatant disregard of justice in Medea's case was sure to anger the gods and Aegeus was quite happy to take the gods' side on this issue. (And he was right – there is no sign then or later that the gods wanted to punish Medea for her revenge. They respected creative nastiness, no matter how nasty it got.)

So it is clear that Aegeus knew what kind of deal he was making. His language makes it plain that he understood that Medea was not simply going to slink out of town - as Seneca later suggested the Corinthians thought she would.

Let there be an outpouring of saucy sharp wit and let the throng jest freely as she passes in silent gloom, she who stole away to wed a foreign husband.

Seneca *Medea* l.113

Silent gloom was not Medea's style, and it seems Aegeus knew it. He didn't know and didn't want to know the details but he correctly guessed the result. Medea was going to leave town as she always did – with her bridges burned and armed men in hot pursuit.

Since Corinth was now repudiating the sanctuary it had previously offered, it must have seemed reasonable to Aegeus that Medea did not want him also to later renege on his offer. So, he was happy to comply when Medea demanded he swear by all the gods, and particularly by Medea's grandfather Helios, that he would 'never cast Medea out while he yet lived.' Given Medea's penchant for extreme misbehaviour this was definitely an oath that lacked a few important sub-clauses. As it transpired, this was not the only major mistake that Aegeus was to make that month, but it was a significant blunder nevertheless.

With her line of escape secured, Medea could move on to the next stage of her preparations. This entailed grovelling to Jason, so she sent her children's nurse to summon the man while she forced herself to appear suitably contrite.

Oh, what a fool I have been to get angry with those who have been giving me good advice.

I've quarrelled with the King and my husband when this royal marriage is for the best. ... The fault is mine for resenting the kindness of the gods, and that at a time when I'm going into exile and need all the friends I can get. ... Now I see that you've acted for the best and instead of being an idiot I should have been there with you, rejoicing in this union.

But you know how we women are. So don't respond badly to my

PREPARATIONS

foolishness, especially as I now see how wrong I was.
Euripides Medea l.882 passim

Contrite as Medea wanted to appear, Jason's smug and patronising reply must have stretched her self-control to the limits.

Well, my dear. I like what I'm now hearing from you. Not that I hold your previous tantrum against you. It's natural for females to get annoyed when their husbands secretly scheme to marry someone else behind their backs. You just needed time to see sense.
(Ibid l.907)

At this point Medea raised the question again of her children. She had to do this delicately - reproaching Jason for his broken promises in this regard would only antagonize him again and undo the work she had put in. She knew that Jason genuinely loved the boys so it would not be hard to persuade him to keep his children with him. The problem was Creon. Therefore, Medea urged Jason 'Beg Creon to spare our boys. Raise them here with your paternal guidance.'

Jason was dubious but agreed that he would try to convince Creon. Medea came up with the helpful suggestion that it would be easier to persuade the king if his own daughter added her prayers to those of Jason. And she had the perfect way to get the daughter onside.

I have a robe which is a gift from the gods, a treasure of my house and kingdom. Helios gave it to Aeëtes as a gift when he became a grandfather. There is also a shining necklace of gold threads and a headband of gold encrusted with sparking gems. My sons can bring these gifts to the bride.

Seneca Medea 1.568

Euripides has Medea continue 'Even the gods are won over by gifts. And when it comes to persuading humans, gold outweighs a thousand words. Ensure that these gifts brought by my children are placed directly in the hands of the bride and in the hands of none other.' By this means, surely the princess would then be persuaded.

By this time Jason should have smelled a rat the size of an elephant. Instead, he appears to have been delighted that things were working out even better than he had hoped. Medea had reconciled herself to being divorced and banished. Better yet she had somehow come to accept Jason's argument that he was doing all this as a favour to her. For Jason the one downside had been that while he was gaining a princess bride Creon was insisting that his beloved children should be exiled – and now here was Medea sacrificing her dearest possessions to make sure that this would not happen. It was just too good to be true.

Jason might have pondered this 'too good to be true' thesis a bit more. But he was in too much of a hurry to get back to his fiancée and let her know that she was about to acquire a pair of step-children. After all, if Jason could convince Medea to feel grateful for the way he had treated her there was clearly no limit to his powers. He should have no problem persuading his young, impressionable bride-to-be to adopt his off-

PREPARATIONS

spring from a former marriage. Things would get even easier when Medea's children showed up to add their boyish pleas to the gifts their mother was even now preparing. Preparing the gifts Medea definitely was. According to Seneca -

She grabs her most lethal herbs, extracts serpents' venom. To this concoction she adds parts of ill-omened birds – an owl's heart and the intestines of a screech-owl, removed while it was yet alive. The Queen of dark magiks carefully lays these objects into separate piles. Here the ravenous power of fire; here the chilling power of icy cold. And no less chilling and fearsome are her incantations. All that is natural shudders as she begins her chant.

Seneca *Medea* 1.731

In fact, for her ingredients Medea needed nothing but readily available mineral ores, lots of seawater (fortunately Corinth had not one, but two seaports), and a very advanced knowledge of chemistry. The magical incantation which Medea chanted would have been roughly along the lines of $2NaCl \rightarrow 2Na + Cl_2\uparrow$ assuming that she was using the standard method of including sodium chloride to extract metallic sodium from seawater. This method requires temperatures of over 600 Celsius (*i.e.*, over 1100 degrees Fahrenheit) but this was little challenge to the grand-daughter of the Sun.

Next came the extraction of magnesium from the same seawater. Magnesium is one of the most abundant elements on the earth's surface, but so reactive it has to be extracted for the pure metal. Then, after adding processed bauxite (available from deposits around Mt Parnassus) with a very exact measure of iron oxide, Medea had enough thermite to reduce her rival princess to powdered ash. 'The ravenous power of fire' indeed. The 'chilling power of cold' was needed not for the thermite itself, but so that Medea's firebomb did not ignite on the spot. To be usable the sodium had to be carefully weakened by the admixture of an inert substance – perhaps chalk or powdered clay.

Remains of a theatre in Sicily where plays such as Seneca's 'Medea' would have been staged (photo Avinash Shah)

Medea was striving for an almost impossibly precise balance. She needed a substance that would not spontaneously combust on exposure to air, but ignite at very low temperature - such as the body heat of an excited princess. This compound had to be smeared on to the inside of the dress, and for that final classy touch of extra malice, perhaps magnesium on the wire which was decoratively entwined with the necklace and ornamentation of the headband?

If Medea had been keeping up with her spell-work while in Corinth – and the legends assure us that she had (everyone needs a hobby) - then most of the preparation had already been done. All that remained was to wrap the gifts in suitable insulation – perhaps a layer of fine suede - and send her sons to join their father on their unwitting mission of murder.

Medea was now set to trash the dress more spectacularly than any bride has managed in the eras since.

Chapter 11

Murder Most Foul
And Character Assassination too

Her children dispatched with the gifts for the princess, Medea could now do nothing but wait. During the waiting Medea appears to have conducted some further negotiations with the gods. The outcome of these negotiations meant that she would need to make an urgent trip to Thebes as soon as her business in Corinth was completed. Still, perilous as it was to be dealing with the dread powers on Olympus, such negotiations were probably better than just sitting and passively awaiting news from the palace of Creon. Whatever news came from there was going to be bad. The best (but improbable) scenarios for her children were that Medea was either about to lose them to Jason or that the children were going to be cast out with her into perilous exile. The more likely scenario was grimmer.

Therefore Medea showed no pleasure when a messenger arrived from the palace to inform her that Jason's bride-to-be had accepted her wedding gifts. This meant that Medea's children were permitted to remain in Corinth and were even now returning to collect their things. Thereafter the children would return to the palace in the certainty that the princess would persuade her father to allow her new step-sons to join the royal household.

Beware of Greek (children) bearing gifts ...

Medea had decidedly mixed feelings as her children re-entered her home a short while later. The acceptance of her gifts by the princess meant that her offspring were to all intents and purposes already dead. Medea knew full well what was happening at the palace at that very moment. And as the instruments who had – however unwittingly - caused the doom of the royal family of Corinth, the children also were doomed. Euripides has Medea torn by grief as she accepts the inevitable consequences of her ghastly plan.

> *I know full well that the royal bride has placed my crown on her head and donned the robe I gave her. She's as good as gone. I'm not going to hand over my children for them* [i.e. the people of Corinth] *to abuse and insult. There's no way that they are not going to die. The question is just who kills them. By the gods, once I had the idea of them nursing me in my old age, and when I passed away their loving hands would lay out my corpse. Well, that sweet dream is dead and gone. Instead I shall lose them in bitterness and sorrow.*
>
> Euripides Medea l.1029ff

Once her children were within her house, Medea settled down to await further news with grim anticipation.

An audience in the ancient world never got to see violence or death portrayed on the stage. Such things were literally obscene, because that's what 'obscene' means. *Ob scena* is the Latin for 'offstage' which is where all the gory stuff happened. What the audience experienced was an account of what had happened elsewhere, and the reactions of the protagonists to the news.

Unconstrained by such conventions, the modern reader can step over to the palace of Creon and observe events directly, while noting that minors will need parental guidance (of the non-Medean variety). This guidance should be used to steer the kids firmly out of the room, because things in Creon's household were about to get decidedly unpleasant.

The opening scene was set about an hour previously.

MURDER MOST FOUL

Things begin innocently enough. The golden-haired children approach the princess with Jason hovering anxiously behind them. The palace servants and Medea's retainers are full of relieved smiles because they have heard that Jason and Medea have patched things up between them.

The princess herself looks eagerly at her husband-to-be, since whatever his faults Jason is certainly eye candy for the discerning female viewer. Yet a certain something has gone – Jason lacks that indefinable aura which he possessed while he was a favourite of the goddess Hera. But Hera is the goddess responsible for the sanctity of marriage – and by his renunciation of Medea, Jason has violated his marriage vows. Consequently Hera has withdrawn her favour.

This matters, a lot, because it will be remembered that over a decade ago Jason murdered the brother of Medea outside the temple on the island of Artemis. This killing unleashed the vengeance of those primal entities, the Furies, who punish crimes perpetrated within the family. Escaping the Furies had forced the Argonauts to make their trans-Mediterranean trip to the magical island of Circe. There Medea's aunt had used her formidable powers to put the vengeance of the Furies on hold - but by their nature the Furies are incapable of forgiving or forgetting. Without Hera's protection, Jason is now vulnerable to their wrath.

Were Hera still favouring Jason one can see how things might go. The princess sees the children and goes pale. She turns her head away in anger at their presence and refuses to look at them again. Perhaps, the goddess Hera willing, the princess will order the children out of her sight and they will be ushered away, returning to Medea with their lethal gifts still clutched in their little hands. Foiled by the goddess Medea storms off into exile vowing later vengeance. This optimal scenario does not happen.

Instead, the princess eyes the presents with wonder while Jason unleashes his considerable powers of persuasion. Medea once commented to Jason, 'In my opinion no-one deserves a heavier penalty than someone who can twist words to support an unjust cause. People like you believe you can veil injustice with words and so you dare to be unjust. Yet specious pleas and clever words may not be so clever after all.'

Medea's reproach is far from Jason's mind as he gives his beloved a honeyed smile and says soothingly. 'Please darling, don't be angry. Look over here, please. You have to consider dear to you those whom your husband holds dear. And look at these gifts! Surely for these it is worth getting your father to lift his decree of exile from my children? Come, do it for me.'

It's an irony that Medea will certainly later appreciate. Here's Medea's revenge against her husband about to be derailed almost before it has started. But no, Jason himself strains his charm to the utmost to put Medea's plans back on track. Medea was never vulnerable to Jason's persuasion but with the princess it works. The girl is determined to be in all ways a good and obedient wife and well, the presents are magnificent – literally gifts from the gods. It's a dowry all the more piquant because it is given by the woman whose man she has taken.

Medea imagines the princess in flames in this excerpt from The Vision of Medea by Joseph Turner (1828)

Euripides takes up the tale (l.1370ff)

As soon as Jason has taken the children from the palace she picks up *the beautifully embroidered gown and puts it on. Then, taking a seat before a bright mirror she places the golden crown upon her head, arranging it in her hair while smiling happily at her unliving reflection. Exulting in the gifts she rises and shows off, parading around the room on her delicate, pale feet, glancing often at the hem that swishes about her ankles. Then, in a moment, this pretty scene changes to horror.*

She goes pale, reels and staggers backward into her chair, almost sliding sideways to the floor. An old servant thinks the princess has been possessed by Pan or some other god and so raises a paean of praise. Then she sees the foam bubbling from the girl's mouth, the eyes rolling and bulging in their sockets and the blood draining fast from her face.

The next cry is of terror, not praise.

Her handmaidens rush off, one to the king's quarters, another after Jason to tell what has befallen his bride. The house is a-clatter with footsteps as people rush to and fro. Yet within the time a speedy person can complete six plethra [about two hundred yards] *the princess revives from her silent trance. Her eyes fly open and she shrieks in agony from twofold pain. The golden diadem on her head has burst into ravening fire, consuming everything nearby, while her fine white flesh is eaten away by that finely woven robe which was the childrens' gift.*

Like a fiery comet she leaps from her chair and as she runs she throws her head violently from side to side seeking to dislodge the golden diadem from her hair. Yet the fastenings hold firm and when she tosses her head the flames roar twice as high.

Overwhelmed by this cruel twist of fate, she sinks to the ground, unrecognisable to any but a parent.

Gone is the clear gaze from those eyes, veiled with rivulets of blood and fire. Her face is a thing of horror, the flesh dribbling from her bones like resin oozing from a pine tree, chewed away by the poison's secret jaws. Everyone is too afraid to touch the corpse for fear of becoming a corpse themselves. And no-one has time to warn that poor wretch, her father, as he rushes unexpectedly into the room, unaware what has become of her until he stumbles over her body. He howls and wraps her in his arms, exclaiming between kisses,

"Oh my poor child, what god has destroyed you in this ghastly way? Who has robbed me of you in my old age, with so few years to enjoy your presence? My child, my child, if only I could die with you!"

Finishing his sad lament he tries to rise, but finds that horrid robe clinging to his body like ivy about a bay tree. A dreadful struggle follows as he tries to stand, but his daughter drags him down. And when he pulls with all his might he pulls the very flesh from his bones. Eventually he succumbs to the awful suffering and breathes his last. So there they lie side by side, the young daughter and aged sire in a scene of tragedy and horror.

With that one ghastly move Medea obtained satisfaction against the woman who had supplanted her and the king who had ordered her exiled. Furthermore, the flames from the immolated princess refused to die even when doused with water. This suggests that Medea had added phosphorus or a solidified naptha product to give the bride's complexion that special glow. (*cf* Macabees 2.20-22 which describes naptha spontaneously combusting in sunlight.)

Because the palace was in total confusion after the unexpected death of the king there was no-one to take charge and the flames rapidly spread from the princess to the room to the building. Eventually the entire palace was ablaze, fulfilling Medea's grim prophecy that the ruin of the house of Creon would be visible as a column of smoke even in the southernmost part of Greece. It was a spectacular revenge which, through its very lack of subtlety, left no-one in doubt of the perpetrator.

At this point all that anyone knew was that the unfortunate princess had spontaneously combusted and her father had perished while unwisely coming into contact with her remains. It might, just perhaps, have been co-incidence that at the time that she ignited the combustee had been wearing clothing donated by Medea, but no-one was buying that for a moment. Medea had publicly vowed comprehensive and horrible vengeance and given her previous reputation, what had just occurred could not be mistaken for anything but Medea delivering on her promises.

Therefore as the news spread among the indignant people of Corinth this was accompanied by a mass movement of the populace towards the house of Medea. Nor were the masses shy about their intentions – this was a lynch mob. As the king of Athens had correctly supposed, Medea was not going to slink quietly out of town into exile. Instead 'escape' was definitely the order of the day.

At the head of this mob was Jason. As soon as Jason

had received news of events at the palace, he set out for Medea. One notes that the hero did not bother rushing back to the palace to see if anything could be retrieved from the disaster. He knew his ex-wife, and Medea was nothing if not thorough. Her revenge would be comprehensive enough to leave nothing of the princess, her father, or as it turned out, of the palace they both shared. All that Jason could do now was make sure that he was at the head of the crowd when they arrived at his former home.

After all, this was not the first royal family that Medea had dispatched - and her earlier assassination had been intended for Jason's benefit. Now with the exception of one Hippotes, the (possibly illegitimate) son of Creon, nothing remained of the immediate Corinthian royal family. This meant Jason, of impeccable royal blood and heroic reputation, was well-placed to assume the throne, especially as his family had historic ties to Corinth. Jason had been conveniently abroad when Medea wiped out much of the royal family of Iolcus – so who could say that his 'estrangement' from Medea on the occasion of her Corinthian massacre was not also part of some cunning plot designed to put Jason in power?

All of this must have occurred in a moment to Jason. However deficient he was in the hero department, Jason was an extremely savvy politician. It would have been immediately apparent to him that the best way to avoid being tarred with the same regicidal brush as Medea was to be at the head of the crowd storming Medea's home. When the crowd started demanding that Medea pay for her crimes, Jason intended to be first among those doing the demanding.

Had events not been so emotionally charged it might have occurred to Jason that ten years of marriage had made him highly predictable to his spouse and in getting to the front of the mob Jason had put himself exactly where Medea expected him to be. It should also have crossed his mind that, if Medea had accomplished so terrible an end for Creon and his daughter, then Medea doubtless had something even worse planned for himself. After all, in Medea's mind Jason was the villain of the piece.

By now Medea was well aware of what had transpired at the palace. Even before the towering plume of smoke from the blazing building had signalled her success Medea had been informed of events by a messenger. This conversation shows again the dark side of Medea's character. When the messenger informs her that the princess and the king are dead, Medea responds, 'You have made a friend by bringing me this news. To become truly dear to me, please tell me that they died in agony.'

This was not the attitude of a women who felt she was going to have soon to plead for her life with the people whose royal family she had just killed. And indeed, Medea was not at all concerned about her personal safety. As we have seen from her discussions with the King of Athens and her subsequent negotiations with the Gods, her revenge was never intended to be a suicide mission.

Like many a young woman of later eras, Medea in her teenage years had been in the habit of borrowing transport from older members of her family. In her case the vehicle in question was the chariot of her grandfather, the sun god Helios. When laying her plans, one of the first things that Medea had checked was that her grandfather was still prepared to make that chariot available. The chariot was now tucked out of sight on the roof, its dragons awaiting passenger boarding for the planned flight to Thebes. There was however a major snag. The chariot could only carry one passenger - and three of those in the house were in mortal danger.

In Corinth Medea was now definitely public enemy number one, but her sons currently held positions two and three. In the world of pre-archaic Greece children were not spared in the cut-throat political and personal rivalries of their elders. When in his madness Hercules had killed his own children, he had actually thought that he was killing the equally young offspring of his rival Eurysthenes. Hercules had to atone for his actions because he had inadvertently killed his own – the children of rivals and enemies were fair game.

While Medea could escape with ease, she could only do so alone and at the price of leaving her children to be torn apart by the Corinthian mob. And the mob would certainly do so. Even if they did not know that it was the children who had given the princess the lethal garments (and by now many in the crowd probably did know) the fact remained that these were the children of Medea. Killing those children would be considered tit-for-tat retaliation for Medea's killing the daughter of their king.

Medea had realized this problem early. Yet this had not changed her plans but had instead become another element to be factored into them. Okay, her children had to die. How could this happen to her maximum advantage? It is to her credit that this was the one part of her revenge which Medea was squeamish about, and to her eternal discredit that she cold-bloodedly went through with it anyway. Back to Euripides (l.1240ff) where she muses ...

Anyone who feels he cannot witness this sacrifice - let such a one imagine how it feels to actually perform it. My hand has the strength for this handiwork yet my heart tells me not to do this murder. Should I spare my children to remain alive with me in Athens, there to make me happy?

Remorseful or no, Medea knows that this is wishful thinking. Matters have moved past the point where she has a choice.

No! By the demons from the depths of the underworld I swear I'll never leave my children to be abused by their enemies. They will be killed, whatever happens. And since there's no getting away from it the mother who gave them life must kill them.

All that remained now was to bid farewell. Kneeling, Medea hugged her children, murmuring,

Now my babes, let your mother kiss those hands I love so well. Ah, those lips, form and features so dear to me. I wish you joy, but in that other land. For here your father has taken away your place. That sweet embrace, the tender skin, the fragrant breath ... Go! Get inside! I can't bear to look at you any more.

At this point the stories of Seneca and Jason diverge again, though in both tellings of the legend, Jason is desperately worried about the children. The extracts below are a synthesis of the different accounts of Euripides and Seneca as each imagined events unfolding.

Where is she, the perpetrator of these ghastly crimes? Still inside or already running for her life? She's going to have to hide in the bowels of the earth or take wings to the roof of heaven if she thinks she will avoid the revenge of the royal house. How does she think that she's going to get away with it? She's killed the ruler of this land!

Yet that's by the by. Those she has wronged are going to do the same to her. I'm here for my children. The family of the victims are going to take their revenge on them – a murder to repay the murder most foul done by their mother.

Jason cannot see what is plain to the magical Medea – over a decade previously the pair had asked Circe to purge them of the blood-guilt incurred by the slaying of Medea's brother. Circe had done her best, but her best had succeeded only in deferring payment for their crimes. The Furies were implacable and unstoppable – and now they were here. It is time for the debt to be repaid. Medea remarks,

And here come the Furies in a headlong onslaught. Against which of us are they lifting their flaming bows? Who are they threatening with those blood-stained torches? … There, behind them I see scattered limbs. Oh yes, my brother is here to witness the punishment. Well, what is owed will be paid, in full. So you want them to stab the brands into my eyes, to tear and burn? Well, by breast is open to their assault.

But peace, my brother. Tell the avenging goddesses to step back. You'll depart sated to join the deep-dwelling spirits below. Make this your hand, brother, with which I have drawn my sword. With this victim I pay my debt!

Medea then launches an attack on one of her sons, who leaps back in terror from her sword. For the next minute or so there follows a horrible game of cat-and-mouse as the terrified children try to escape their suddenly murderous mother. They dodge around the furniture, calling to one another as they try to figure out why the mother who was so loving just a moment ago has abruptly turned on them with murder in mind. Inevitably, one finally cries out 'I'm trapped! She's got me!'

At this point the mob arrives with Jason at its head, with Medea's ex-husband loudly making clear that he is on the side of truth, light and justice.

Loyal citizens who grieve for your slain princess! Follow me and let's capture the author of this dreadful crime. Here! Here, my brave band of warriors! Take to arms and let's burn this house to the foundations. ... See, there she is herself, leaning over the roof's edge. Someone bring a torch, so that as she falls she also can die in flames!

Those looking up at the sneering face of Medea can hardly guess at the emotions tearing through her. She is wracked with guilt for the son she has killed and anguished at the thought of killing the other. Yet there is also a kind of dreadful triumph as she sees Jason leading the mob, just where she wanted and expected him to be. A fierce delight surges up through her as she sees him stop in appalled horror as she lifts the bloody corpse of their dead son. 'If only' she thinks, 'Like Niobe, I had a brood of twelve children. Two is just not enough to do this job properly.'

Mommy dearest

To Jason's greater horror, he sees that there's still one

of his sons alive – but now Medea has her sword at his throat while the boy squirms in terror.

Jason: *By all the gods, for the sake of who we were when we fled from Colchis together, by our marriage bed, I beg you spare the boy. If there is any guilt, I'm the guilty one. You want a death, I'll give myself up. Let it be on my head.*

Medea: *Oh, I'm going to stab you, all right. My sword point goes here, where it will hurt you the most. Then you can take your self-righteous self off again to marry a maid and abandon her when she's a mother.*

Jason: *One death is enough punishment.*

Medea: *If I was going to stop at one, I'd never have started at all. As it is, if I thought a trace of your seed remained within me, I'd search out my own guts with this sword.*

Jason: *And you torture me still with this suspense. Well, I'm done begging.*

Medea: *You're not in control here Jason. I'm doing things at my own pace. Revenge is best taken slow. But as you wish …* [With one thrust she kills the boy]. *Well, it's done. What now Jason? Do you now want to recognize me as your wife?*

Jason: *You bitch! The gods and all mankind have to hate you for this. You, the mother who gave them birth, killing your own sons.*

Look what you have done to me – I'm left destroyed and childless! After what you've done, how can you still look on the earth and sun? I hope both are your ruin! I must have been mad to bring you here to a Greek home. You. A savage from a savage land. You were evil even then. Oh yes, you betrayed father and fatherland, killed your brother. And the Furies meant for your punishment have claimed me instead. You bore my children only because you lusted for sex in the marriage bed. That's why you could kill them. No Greek woman would dare. No, not any woman would dare. You're not a woman. You're a she-lion, more bestial than any monster.

You killed them.

... But did she?

Everyone who knows of Medea knows this of her. She was a woman who would go to any lengths to revenge herself on the man who had spurned her, even if that revenge meant she had to kill her own children just to hurt him. Such an act requires either an almost inconceivable degree of emotional intensity or the unfeeling calculation of a psychopath.

Euripides, in a brilliant bit of playwriting, manages to square the circle and have Medea be an anguished mother and a cold-blooded killer at the same time. It is this superb management of the narrative that makes Medea's actions stand out as much as the nature of the crime itself. In itself, Medea's behaviour seems far less egregious when placed alongside the many other horrors which abound in the grim world of Greek mythology. Indeed one of the things which makes

Medea's murders stand out is that they are human enough to be imaginable while some of the other misdeeds of myth are so outré that the imagination struggles to encompass their enormity.

Unless one reads the bowdlerized modern versions adapted for children, mythical misbehaviour starts right at the beginning of the corpus with the incest of Gaia and Uranus. This is swiftly followed by Cronus castrating his father and later eating his own children. Things pretty much go downhill from there by way of rape, bestiality, fratricide, matricide, patricide, sororicide and infanticide. So what makes Medea's case so special?

This brings us back to Euripides. Seneca portrays Medea as an unfeeling monster who revels in the blood she is shedding and the pain that she causes. For Seneca, Medea is just another of those hideous creatures of myth, like the half-woman, half-snake Echidna, like the Harpies or the child-devouring Lamia. If that really was all there is to Medea we could read the story and pass on with a quick shudder. That's what we do with the story of Tantalus, who not only killed his son, but then served him up for dinner. Yet we pause at Medea. No-one has written epic plays about the ghastly Tantalus, but there are several about Medea, and this is because of Euripides. He made Medea human and her actions understandable, if not forgiveable.

The Medea of Euripides is no creature of myth – it's someone with whom, in our darker moments we can identify. It is certainly not unheard of in the modern era for one parent to kill his or her children to hurt a spouse. In fact modern psychiatry even has a name for the impulse – it's called the Medea Complex (naturally). The fact is though, that these modern murderers have much less excuse than Medea. She knew that what she had already done meant that her children were doomed – and in her warped perception, if the boys had to die it was better that the deed be be done, not by strangers but by someone who loved them even as she killed them.

The Medea of Euripides really, really wants to have a heart of stone, but instead she in anguished and torn with guilt. She has to force herself every step of the way, taking us along with her as we will her to stop and reconsider. Yet she does not – and defying all modern convention – once she has committed her murders, Medea gets away with it. Why?

Jason curses Medea as hateful in the sight of gods and men for her crime, yet by and large neither gods nor men agreed with him, either then or in later antiquity. Certainly what Medea had done was seen as a brutal, shameful deed. But not an inexcusable one. To understand why, we need to abandon our modern mindset and see things from the very different perspective of the classical era.

In the modern era we associate death with old age. In the ancient world, death came for the children. This started at childbirth, which was so perilous that the Spartans ranked a woman who had given birth with the social standing equivalent of a man who had completed a season of active duty in the army. (In fact Euripides has Medea snarl that she would sooner face a hundred spears than give birth just once.)

A newborn child came into a world which was innocent of some basic ideas of hygiene and bereft of vaccinations or antibiotics. Many children were born into cities so unhealthy – even without the periodic plagues – that they were net consumers of people and needed to be constantly refreshed by immigration from the countryside. It is estimated that up to three out of every five children perished before they reached adolescence. This extreme casualty rate hardened the people of the ancient world to the death of children to an extent unimaginable in the modern west.

As a result, even if they survived birth, infection and disease, children of the classical world faced another danger – their own parents. Abortion was rare and dangerous so most parents preferred to let an unwanted baby come to term before they killed or otherwise disposed of it. In many ancient cities there were places set aside for the disposal of unwanted babies. In Rome it was the Forum Holitorum, in Athens near one of the city gates. Here the children were placed on the ground to either be picked up by anyone looking to adopt, or to die of hunger and exposure. Other babies were simply dumped on garbage heaps.

In a letter which has survived from the Roman era, a husband writes fondly to his wife. He enquires how matters stand at home and then adds, 'You tell me that you are pregnant again. If it is a boy, keep him, if it's a girl, kill it.' In Roman law a father had the power of *patria potestas*, which meant that he could legally execute a child – or whatever age – if he so pleased and do so with complete impunity. In short, the killing of children was seen as nowhere near as dreadful a deed as we consider it today. Even when Jason yells to Medea 'No Greek woman would dare to do this!' he does not mean that no Greek woman would kill her child. He means that no Greek woman would dare to do it without first asking her husband's permission.

When it came to transgressing societal norms, Jason was considered at fault as much as Medea. In the modern world many a divorce occurs because one of the other spouse thinks they have found a better partner. In ancient Greece this sort of conduct was a more serious offence, because of the extreme vulnerability of the abandoned wife. This was even more so in the case of Medea who had no family to support her after the divorce and no place to go once she had been exiled. As the writer Diodorus Siculus has remarked, 'Meanwhile ... everyone agrees that with the loss of his wife and children Jason had only suffered what coming to him.' (Diod. 4.55.1)

This callousness on Jason's part is why Helios was prepared to provide a getaway vehicle for a child-killer and why Aegeus, king of Athens, was prepared to offer her sanctuary afterwards. Medea was considered almost as much a victim as were her children, so she could literally get away with murder – if she did indeed commit those murders. She may not have done. There exists a very solid case whereby it could be argued that in fact it is Euripides whodunnit.

Did Euripides invent the case against Medea? Exhibit A in the case for the prosecution comes in the form of an obscure type of antique writings called scholia. Scholia are not actual texts *per se*, but are annotations appended to ancient works of literature by scholars of antiquity and of the Byzantine era. Almost as soon as the ink was dry on the text of Euripides the first scholia appeared alongside it, noting where Euripides had taken liberties with his subject matter (something he did a lot) or simply adding commentary or footnotes to the main text. Modern researchers have painstakingly gleaned these scholia from various manuscripts and published them as separate texts. The one which particularly interests us is called the *Scholia in Euripidem*. In this text various ancient experts in matters mythical haul Euripides over the coals for his sensationalist treatment of Medea.

Here is the 'real' account of events according to one Didymus, an academic of the first century BC. (scholion l.264 ibid) who has for his source an even earlier epic poet from Samos (date unknown) called Kreophylus.

According to Kreophylus, Medea did kill Creon and his daughter as described. Again as described by Euripides, Medea knew that she could only escape at the cost of abandoning her children. However in the older, pre-Euripidean, accounts that is exactly what Medea did. When her children returned home after delivering their deadly presents to the palace Medea did not sit about awaiting developments as Seneca and Euripides report. Instead she rushed to the Heraion of Perachora, and deposited her children there.

This Heraion of Perachora needs a bit of explanation. Corinth straddles an isthmus between two seas - the Saronic gulf in the east, and the Gulf of Corinth to the west. Perachora (literally 'the land beyond') was a small peninsula on the western side of the city. In a cove on the peninsula was a fishermen's harbour and a small temple/shrine to Hera. Such shrines were known as 'Heraions'. Medea's choice of this location was very deliberate. Hera was the goddess of marriage, and in breaking the oaths which he had sworn at his nuptials, Jason had broken the oaths he had sworn to Hera. If any of the Olympian gods were going to see the justice of Medea's subsequent actions, that would be Hera, so Medea trusted the goddess with the safety of her children. Nevertheless, she did not trust the goddess so far that she did not choose an obscure and out-of-the way hiding spot.

There is an apocryphal account that once she had reached this location Medea over-reached herself by trying to put a spell of inviolability on the Heraion. Somehow the spell went wrong and it triggered a small landslide in which the children perished.

Anyone visiting the Heraion today can see how this might happen. The cove is still there, as is the Heraion, though the latter is now in ruins. The sacred spot is located on a ledge above a narrow beach, with low but steep cliffs curving behind and on either side. It is not hard to imagine a rogue spell bringing down a section of cliff-side right upon a group of huddled children. (According to the scholia Medea had fourteen children, but Euripides drastically pruned their number to avoid a very repetitive bloodbath.)

This makes the death of the children a tragic accident. Though Medea remains the killer, by this telling the killings were inadvertent and happened in the course of Medea's attempts to secure the children's safety - which puts a very different complexion on matters. However Parmeniskos a grammarian of the early first century BC, goes even further, exonerating Medea completely. (Of killing her own children, that is. No-one doubts that she killed Creon and his daughter.)

MEDEA, QUEEN OF WITCHES

According to Parmeniskos (scholia to l. 264) the women of Corinth pursued the children of Medea to the Heraion and found them clasping the altar as supplicants. This did not save the children because the enraged Corinthians went right ahead and slit the children's throats anyway, regardless of the sanctity of that sacred place. A further addendum to the text relates that the killers were the relatives of Creon, literally out for blood.

Such violations of a temple were not treated lightly by the deity to whom the place was sacred. Hera was already somewhat peeved with the Corinthians because their king had encouraged Jason to violate the marriage vows made in her name. When the people of the city went even further by killing children who had fled to her sanctuary, the outraged Hera took this as a declaration of war. She turned to her step-son Apollo. Today Apollo is considered the god of music and the fine arts but it should be remembered that his name comes from the ancient Anatolian 'Apolydon' - the destroyer.

Destroying is exactly what Apollo settled down to do. As he was to do a generation later in the camp of the Greeks at Troy, his chosen weapon was plague. At Troy also, Apollo's motivation was the violation of a temple (and the kidnapping of a priest's daughter). With their citizens dropping like flies, the Corinthians sued for peace. Hera's terms were that every year seven boys and seven girls from the city's most noble families had to spend a year serving the goddess at the place which they had so brutally violated.

This seems to be more or less confirmed in a slightly different account by the Greek travel writer Pausanias, who visited Corinth in Roman times - almost a millennium after the events described here. Describing his visit to Corinth (Pausanias *Guide to Greece* 2.3.6ff) the writer tells of being taken to Perachora and shown ...

... the Tomb of Medea's children. It is said they were stoned to death by the Corinthians because of the gifts which they had borne to the princess. These deaths were violent and unjust. Because of this, plague killed all newborn Corinthians until they consulted an oracle. At the oracle's command a warning statue was erected. This is in the form of a terrifying woman [a vengeful Medea, or a furious Hera?] *and it survives to this day. After the Romans sacked Corinth and destroyed the former population, the new inhabitants no longer perform the expiatory sacrifices and their children do not cut their hair in mourning or wear dark clothing.*

The point is that, even in historical times, the Corinthians were purging their guilt for killing Medea's children. The rituals for so doing are reported by as about as reliable a source as we get for the ancient world. Since the Corinthians doing penance for the killings, this means that they were very probably guilty of the killings. There's no point in repenting something you haven't done. In terms of killing her offspring then, Medea is off the hook. So why does Euripides claim that Medea did the deed, and say so in a play of such epic power that his account has supplanted all previous versions of the myth?

The *Medea* was written in 431 BC, a date significant because this was the year in which began the

MEDEA, QUEEN OF WITCHES

Peloponnesian War, a savage multi-nation conflict which was to convulse the cities of Greece for decades to come. With the war about to kick off, all factions were seeking to gather allies and isolate their enemies. Therefore the Corinthians were not best pleased that one of the foremost playwrights in Greece was about to stage a performance which depicted them as the killers of Medea's children. In religious terms the Corinthians and their Spartan allies were eager to recruit Apollo to their cause. Consequently the Corinthians were not really keen to remind the deity that they had been on the receiving end of his wrath in earlier centuries.

The problem for the Corinthians was that they were part of the pro-Spartan faction opposed to the rise of Athens. Therefore they could hardly appeal to the Athenian Euripides that his play was putting them in a bad light at a critical time. Instead they chose a different means of persuasion.

The scholion to line 9 of the play notes that an ancient academic called Mousaios wrote a text called 'The Isthmia'. In this Mousaios explains the 'rites of Hera Akraia' – presumably those rites of expiation performed by the Corinthians. The scholion also notes that Euripides transferred the charge of murder from the Corinthians to Medea. 'While in fact it was the Corinthians who did the murders while they were enraged.' However, Euripides' radical change to the established myth was accomplished by five talents of Corinthian silver – or to put it another way, the playwright received just over 150 kg (331lbs) of very persuasive bullion to make Medea the guilty party in his play. A rower in the Athenian fleet could expect wages of around a drachma a day, so the payout to Euripides was the equivalent of 30,000 days work. Not bad for one play.

The Athenians were naturally not best pleased with Euripides' re-interpretation of the plot. They showed their feelings by awarding Euripides last place for his masterpiece at the Great Dionysia, the venue of the theatrical competition where the *Medea* of Euripides was first staged. To be fair, though the *Medea* is a powerful piece of writing, there are clearly places where Euripides had to forcibly adjust his plot lines to the new ending. The Athenians – keen connoisseurs of theatre - would have seen and penalized these structural flaws even if they had not been deeply annoyed that this new version had been purchased with Corinthian silver.

The Athenians seem to have carried their grudge. It is reported that of the 72 plays Euripides wrote in his career only 19 thereafter won prizes. This, despite the massive renown of the playwright outside Athens. Nor did the attacks on his character let up. Euripides was (falsely) accused of misogyny and (justly) accused of lewd and unwonted interference with ancient myths and current morality. He was mercilessly lampooned by comics and satirical writers.

One such hit piece, contained within the *Frogs* of Aristophanes survives today. Among a flurry of other sarcastic slurs one character seems to take a dig at Euripides for accepting bribes. 'Euripides is a cunning rogue and he'll try a thousand tricks to get away. But he was easy here, and he'll be easy there'.

'There' was in the underworld of Hades because Euripides had died in the previous year. According to ancient sources, he tired of the relentless mockery and persecution of the Athenians and took himself to the court of the king of Macedon where he felt that would be better appreciated. (At the time the Macedonian king was trying to overcome his nation's philistine reputation by recruiting artistic talent wherever he could find it.)

Sadly Euripides did not long enjoy the amenities of life in Macedonia. Accounts of his death are unclear. The most widely credited tale in antiquity is that, while returning home after a dinner party, he was attacked by a pack of savage Molossian hounds and torn to pieces. The hounds were said to have been unleashed by two rival poets who resented the arrival of Euripides. But one notes that the dogs which killed Euripides are the totemic animal of Medea's aunt and tutor, the goddess Hecate.

Chapter 12

Aftermath

With Medea's flight from Corinth, the two best-known chapters of her life come to an end.

It is significant that with her departure from Corinth Medea steps out of mainstream myths, because this is the point where the average Greek woman ceased to be. Generally speaking, the stage after being a *gyne* was to become a corpse. It is hard for us to estimate across this distance of time with evidence as scanty as we currently possess but it would be fair to state that the life expectancy of a Greek woman in the late bronze age was considerably less than fifty years - and by now Medea was approaching forty.

It is also fair to state that Medea was very far from being an average Greek woman. Her story continues well after that average Greek woman had been laid to rest. However, while she remains as lethal as ever, for the rest of her career Medea is something of a non-person. It is almost as if, after escaping the Corinthian mob in her dragon-powered chariot, Medea is supposed to ride off into the sunset of infamy, never to be heard from again. And indeed, once she has escaped from Corinth this is exactly the point at which many of the accounts of the life of Medea come to an end. From what we can establish, the rest of her story is perhaps even more dramatic than events so far – but no-one bothered to tell it.

A vase from the late 5th century BC shows Medea escaping on her dragon chariot while an appalled Jason sees the bodies of his slain children. Note the winged Furies behind both Jason and Medea.

Instead, the plot must be gleaned from the throwaway comments and off-hand remarks of various classical authors, contradictory as they are, and downright wrong as others must be.

For example, consider the report of Diodorus Siculus, a writer of the first century BC. His famous *Bibliotheca* (part 4.54) tells us that immediately on leaving Corinth, Medea went to Thebes. This agrees with other accounts and also with the negotiations that Medea conducted with the gods prior to obtaining her getaway chariot. The purpose of the visit was to see Hercules.

But according to Diodorus, this was because Hercules had met Medea in Colchis when she was preparing to flee with Jason. In this version Hercules had promised to help Medea if Jason ever violated his oath to 'keep her as his life's companion for so long as he lived'. However, when Medea got to Thebes from Corinth, Hercules turned out to be unable to help Medea because he was insane from the madness which had just caused him to kill his children. Consequently, Medea used her skill with herbs to cure Hercules and then went on her way.

There are all sorts of problems with this account. For a start, everyone but Diodorus reports that when he killed his children Hercules had suffered a temporary (if very bloody) bout of madness from which he returned to sanity on his own accord. Secondly, Diodorus thinks that Hercules and Medea first met in Colchis, which they didn't. And if they had, it would have been after Hercules had stolen the girdle of the Amazonian queen several stages into the Labours by which he expiated the killing of his children while insane. In other words, according to Diodorus, when she arrived in Thebes from Corinth, Medea cured Hercules of a madness from which he must have already recovered at least a decade previously.

This blunder by Diodorus is typical of the anomalies which plague the story of Medea's life from here onward. It does no harm to assume that Medea did meet Hercules in Thebes and cure him of some nameless malady. Several gods were favourably inclined towards Hercules and would have wanted to see him well again. In healing Hercules Medea repaid the service she owed to the gods for the supply of her chariot and for the purging of any guilt she carried for the killing of Creon and his daughter. (One notes that had Medea really killed her own children the cost of expiation would have been much higher – after all Hercules had to perform his twelve famous Labours to get off the hook for the same crime.)

Had Medea and Hercules paired up when they did finally meet in Thebes the results might have written a whole new corpus of myths. Hercules was certainly no mere muscular idiot, but he was definitely muscular, very muscular, and consequently tended to resolve problems with brute force because that is what worked for him. Medea was slightly built and solved problems with magic combined with ruthless intelligence. As a team the pair had complementary skills which might have enabled them to conquer the world - if they could have avoided killing each other first. Both had strong personalities and were deadly when crossed.

As it was, when the deadliest man in myth met the deadliest woman in myth, each recognized the other's lethal potential and behaved with the extreme caution that one reserves today for unexploded bombs. Medea remained in the company of Hercules for several months which must have been a considerable strain upon the nerves of both. Nevertheless, Hercules and Medea kept it calm and professional, completed their business and parted, never to meet again.

Diodorus goes on to describe what became of Jason. 'Unable to cope with the magnitude of the disaster which had befallen him, he committed suicide'. (Diod 4.55.1) This constituted a suitably unheroic end for the least heroic of heroes. Certainly, Medea's revenge had been every bit as effective as she had planned. In a few short hours Jason had lost his children, his wife, his fiancée, his royal sponsor Creon, and his divine protector Hera.

What perhaps hurt even more was that Jason also lost his good standing with the people of Corinth. They regarded him as being in large part responsible for the disaster which had befallen their state. Had Jason not conspired with Creon to divorce Medea, Corinth would not have lost their king and his daughter along with their royal palace. Nor would the state now be enduring a succession crisis. So, where the former golden boy of the legendary Argonauts had once found ready welcome, doors were instead slammed in his face.

It certainly did not help that Jason had been abandoned by Hera – and that he had been abandoned by his divine protector was self-evidently manifest in the misfortunes which currently beset him. Alone and friendless, and probably with money troubles also, Jason is envisaged by Euripides as retreating into the past. He spent his days on the beach beside the decaying hulk of the *Argo*, dreaming of the heroic days of his youth and his adventures with the Argonauts.

One day, as he retreated into the shade of the *Argo* to avoid the midday sun, that ship's legendary oak prow from Dodona – now long silent and rotted through – dropped and crushed him. The fact that Jason was killed by a wooden beam that had originally been contributed by Zeus from his sacred grove might also be an indication that at the time of his unlamented demise the hero's standing with the gods was about as low as it was with the people of Corinth.

Jason had never been a conventional hero. In his day the term 'hero' meant 'leader of a warband'. (The feminine of that title was 'Hera' meaning something approximating to 'lady'.) Rather like the bearers of the title 'Sir' in the Middle Ages, there was something of an accepted standard of behaviour for such people. Heroes were focused on glory – the greater a hero's reputation the more heroic he was meant to be. This was seen as a zero-sum game. One hero gaining glory diminished the standing of the others by comparison. So we see Hercules, for example, hunting down one of his colleagues with homicidal intent because during the successful storming of a city that rival hero had the temerity to gain the glory of being first over the walls. The heroes of myth had great regard for concepts like teamwork, ethics and fair play – as long as they were practised by others.

Jason is unique in being a hero who consulted with his colleagues and occasionally stepped back from the limelight. He actively avoids conflict. As a result, in modern times he is viewed more sympathetically than he deserves.

For a start, while Jason is remembered as the leader of the Argonauts, examples of his actual leadership are hard to find. The ship appears to mostly have been run by committee. Secondly, Jason's usual method of avoiding conflict was to offer up Medea as a sacrifice instead – unless at the time he needed Medea to do his dirty work for him. At their final meeting Jason had the gall to accuse Medea of betraying her family and homeland, conveniently overlooking that Medea had suffered considerable personal sacrifice for doing this - purely for Jason's benefit.

Overly macho testosterone-fuelled heroes may not be admired as they once were – but a conniving selfish wimp with a penchant for back-stabbing is no role model either. It is worth noting that at the time of his death no-one seems to have regretted Jason's passing, let alone vowed to avenge Medea's treatment of him.

Medea meanwhile proceeded from Thebes to Athens where King Aegeus rolled out the welcome mat as he had promised. Aegeus was rather a formidable character in his own right. He was born in the town of Megara in Attica where his family had taken refuge after a usurper had driven them from their ruling position in Athens. With the help of his brothers Aegeus reclaimed the throne by force and then shared with those brothers the rule of Attica. Thus began the process of consolidating Attica into a single city-state (*polis*) of which Athens was the capital.

While Medea had been tending Hercules in Thebes, Aegeus had been busy (Indeed, one suspects that the myth of Medea's Theban interlude was chronologically necessary just to delay her arrival in Athens until Aegeus returned to this home.) When we last met him, Aegeus was in Corinth on his way to consult the learned King of Trozen about the meaning of advice he had received from the Oracle at Delphi – advice that Medea had readily interpreted as being 'Don't screw around until you get home.'

Aegeus promptly ignored that advice and impregnated the King of Trozen's daughter. When the pregnancy began to show Aegeus left his host in a hurry while the embarrassed King tried to convince everyone that his daughter had been impregnated by the God Poseidon. (Plutarch *Life of Theseus* 6). Before he departed for Athens, Aegeus showed his pregnant lover a large boulder beneath which he had deposited his sword and sandals. Aegeus informed the girl that when her son came of age he should move aside the stone, retrieve the items beneath and come to Athens to claim his patrimony. (Interestingly, it seems not for a moment to have occurred to Aegeus that he might have a daughter.)

From there Aegeus completed his journey to Athens. On his return he encountered both the supplicant Medea and envoys from Hippotes, the son of Creon who was indignantly demanding that Medea be returned to Corinth to pay for her crimes. True to the promise he had made in Corinth, Aegeus refused to surrender Medea. Diodorus Siculus reports, 'According to some writers she was put on trial and found not guilty of the charges he [Hippotes] had brought against her.' (Diod 4.55.5)

Clearly this trial was whatever the polar opposite of a kangaroo court might be, but it is nevertheless of note that Aegeus reckoned that there was a case to be presented in Medea's defence. The pro-Medean bias of the Athenian court can be taken as read, but Aegeus clearly felt that Medea would also win in the court of public opinion. Otherwise, he would simply have sent the envoy of Hippotes home with a flat refusal to even consider the request for extradition.

With Medea declared innocent by a court of law and Aegeus still enthusiastically in search of further offspring there was no impediment to Medea and Aegeus becoming king and wife. What became of the previous wife of Aegeus, a woman called Chalciope, is unknown. Interestingly, Medea's sister had that name. So, it may be that Aegeus swapped the elder daughter of Aeëtes for a younger daughter of proven fertility. If that was the case, then Chalciope returned to her deposed father – and indeed some texts have her sharing in his exile.

However, there were several other Chalciopi kicking around in ancient Greece at this time. (It was evidently a popular name.) If the ex-wife of Aegeus was not the sister of Medea, then her fate is unknown. On Medea's arrival in Athens, Chalciope may have perished suddenly (but not unexpectedly) from unknown causes. Or Aegeus might have divorced her, though this is unlikely. Medea had publicly raved about the injustice of Jason abandoning his wife because he had found a better match and Medea had used that injustice as her defence against the charge of murder. Therefore, it would be massively hypocritical for her to then go on to marry another man who had done the exactly same thing to his wife simply because in this case she was the 'better match'.

The best-case scenario is that this Chalciope had already passed away from natural causes before Medea even arrived in Athens. Certainly, there is a story to be told of how Medea came to replace Chalciope, if only the ancient sources had been interested in telling it.

Once the pair were married, our sources are vague about how many children Medea delivered to keep her promise to Aegeus. It seems most likely that there were two – one was named Medus after his mother and the other Perses after his great-uncle. Great-uncle Perses was the man who had deposed his brother Aeëtes from the throne of Colchis, so it appears that in naming her child after this man Medea was hoping for a rapprochement with the ruling family in her homeland. Again, our sources are murky, but we can assume from Medea's later actions that Perses wanted nothing to do with her or her eponymous offspring. This was a mistake, as it had already been demonstrated that Medea did not take rejection well.

This diplomatic rebuff from Colchis notwithstanding, it appears that Medea spent the next eighteen or so years applying the lessons she had learned in Corinth. She was a good Greek wife and properly subservient to her husband - not least because her husband was not stupid enough to demand of her anything she did not feel like being subservient about.

While the marital affairs of Aegeus were peaceful, the rest of kingdom was not. The formerly independent towns of Attica did not like being jammed into a single polity and the people were restless. 'Public affairs were filled with confusion and dissent' says the biographer Plutarch (*Theseus* 12). It did not help that while Aegeus had been childless the sons of his brothers had confidently expected to inherit Attica and divide rule of the place between themselves. The arrival of Medea and her two subsequent children had deeply dismayed them, but they had not completely given up hope of ruling.

It was probably these treasonous nephews who were behind the imprecations of a priestess of Artemis who publicly railed against Medea. This priestess announced to whomever would listen that Medea was a sorceress and a murderer. She claimed that while Medea was in the Athenian state King Aegeus could not conduct an unpolluted sacrifice. This was important, because a polluted sacrifice was slightly worse than no sacrifice at all and without the King doing his due diligence before the gods the whole of Athens was imperilled. It also meant that if Medea was not a legitimate consort of the king, then her children had no standing. Therefore, the claims of the royal nephews could be reinstated.

One can imagine how Medea felt about this. The priestess was able to get away with undermining the legitimacy of Medea's children partly because Medea had learned patience over the years and partly because, however much she might dislike the woman, the priestess was nevertheless a servant of Artemis, a Goddess whom she offended at her peril. The treacherous nephews were another matter but again Medea stayed her hand. Her previous murders of royalty had led to nothing but trouble, so this time Medea was determined to be a good Greek wife, grit her teeth and let Aegeus handle things.

To his credit, Aegeus did exactly that more or less successfully for almost two decades until a new problem turned up. This problem was called Theseus. He was the son conceived through Aegeus' romance with the daughter of the King of Trozen. As Aegeus had intended, when this youth had grown to a man's estate his mother had taken him to the boulder beneath which Aegeus had concealed his sandals and sword. Theseus rolled the boulder aside effortlessly and claimed the symbols of his patrimony. Thereafter the young man set out on the road for Athens and glory.

Glory was very much what Theseus was aiming for. The easy way to get to Athens was to take a boat across the Saronic Gulf, but where was the fun in that? Instead, Theseus set out to make the much slower and more perilous journey by land.

MEDEA, QUEEN OF WITCHES

A very lifelike and remarkably unheroic-looking Theseus is depicted here in this fresco from Pompeii.

In those days there were men who were cunning with their hands and fleet of foot, with indefatigable energy and body strength. But instead of putting these abilities to decent or useful purposes they delighted in using their strength with monstrous arrogance to reap a harvest of cruelty and pain. Everything that came their way they coerced or destroyed. They thought that ordinary men believed in justice, compassion and righteous reverence for the gods because they were too cowardly to act otherwise and lacked the strength to exercise power over others.

Plutarch *Theseus* 6

It was exactly for the purpose of removing such blots from the landscape that heroes such as Hercules existed. The problem was that there was a very thin line separating heroes like Hercules from the villains they were meant to be eliminating. As a case in point, Hercules was unavailable for hero duties at that moment because he was currently elsewhere serving out his sentence for a particularly gratuitous murder. As someone who had long admired Hercules, Theseus was more than happy to fill the vacancy that his hero's absence had created.

The path of young Theseus between Trozen and Athens became strewn with the bodies of miscreants whom the aspiring hero left in his wake. These deaths were a catalogue of ingenious sadism, because Theseus carefully applied to each man the same fate that they were fond of inflicting on others. So, Sinis the Pine Bender was torn apart by the same trees that he used to dismember his victims (for good measure Theseus raped his daughter as well). Sciron was tossed off the cliff from which he was wont to hurl travellers and Termerus, the head-basher, got his skull bashed in.

Procrustes was infamous for wanting people to exactly fit the bed he had prepared for them, even if this meant lopping off any legs that were too long or stretching those who were too short on a rack. (In the early modern era this led to the adjective 'Procrustean' being applied to any one-size-fits-all regime.) Naturally Theseus demonstrated how barbaric this behaviour was by doing the same thing to Procrustes. And so on through a dozen or so other predators upon peaceful travellers.

Thereafter Theseus arrived in Athens having paused along the way at the river Cephistus where he underwent purification rituals for the blood shed over the course of his corpse-littered journey. The entire city was in a hubbub about the arrival of this young man whose reputation had preceded him. Perhaps the only person who was totally unimpressed by Theseus was Medea, who knew trouble when she saw it. With her magical ability she also immediately realized that the new arrival was a son of Aegeus and correctly inferred from this that Aegeus had not heeded the warning of the Oracle of Delphi not to have sex before he got home to Athens. The King's failure to control his libido had become a mortal threat to his well-being - and anything that threatened Aegeus was also a threat to Medea.

As ever when Medea felt threatened, she fell back upon murder as a first resort. Theseus, with a politician's timing, was waiting for when he could reveal his origins at the most dramatic moment. So for now, as far as Aegeus was concerned, Theseus was simply a young hero who had turned up in town riding a wave of public adulation. It was not hard for Medea to explain that someone who commanded that degree of public support was a danger to the already unstable rule of Aegeus – all the easier, in fact, because this was the plain truth. Medea went on to explain that it would be

AFTERMATH

sad but understandable if the young man's exertions along the coastal road on his way to Athens had overtaxed his body. The stress on the poor fellow's metabolism might well cause him to collapse and die – possibly even at a banquet arranged by the King.

The banquet was duly arranged with Theseus as the guest of honour. There Aegeus handed his guest a goblet of wine prepared by Medea, still unaware that it was his own son to whom he was offering a carefully-concocted heart attack in a cup. As guest of honour, it fell to Theseus to carve the roast boar being served to those at the table. This was the perfect time for the big reveal. Theseus dramatically drew his sword to do the slicing, holding the weapon significantly poised while he prepared to take a swig of wine. As Theseus fully intended, Aegeus immediately recognized his own sword and put two and two together. Before Theseus could take his first swallow of wine the King lunged across the table and knocked the goblet from his son's hand. Thereafter all went as Theseus had hoped. 'After questioning his son Aegeus embraced him and then formally acknowledged him before an assembly of the Athenians who happily received him into the citizenry because of his valiant deeds.' (Plutarch *Theseus* 12)

That joyful family reunion completed, Aegeus went on to have a much less happy conversation with his wife. In vain Medea tried to explain that, however heroic his aspect, Theseus was a menace to mankind in general and Aegeus in particular. Aegeus was besotted with the discovery that he had not only an adult son but one who was a *bona fide* hero as well. He was indignant that Medea had attempted to murder his golden boy and deeply alarmed by the revelation the

MEDEA, QUEEN OF WITCHES

Medea was determined to try again at the first opportunity. Recognizing that he and his wife had irreconcilable differences about Theseus surviving to the end of the week, Aegeus felt he had no choice but to order Medea out of Athens with immediate effect.

So Medea became *persona non grata* in Athens just as she had become in Colchis, Iolcus and Corinth. Aegeus had learned the lesson from Medea's other bloody expulsions. His wife was not simply thrown out of Athens, she was provided with an escort and a ship to take her to wherever she wanted to go – and ordered to go immediately, now, and at once. Her luggage would follow. With the example of Creon of Corinth burning brightly in his memory, Aegeus had no intention of allowing Medea even a single minute for vengeful scheming.

Rather to his surprise, Medea meekly departed. Aegeus would have been somewhat less reassured if he had also remembered that in Corinth he had sworn a binding oath in the name of several gods that he would never cast out Medea in the exact manner that he was now casting her out. Medea did not need to harm Aegeus – he had doomed himself twice over; once when he ignored the warning of the Delphic Oracle and again when he broke his oath to Medea.

It took about a year, which by the timetable of the immortal gods was reasonably prompt. Theseus was determined to travel to Crete and slay the dreaded Minotaur, despite the anguish that Aegeus felt at the possibility of losing his beloved son. Aegeus assured Theseus that every day he would be at the clifftop at Sunion waiting for early news of how the monster-slaying attempt had gone. If the deed was done

AFTERMATH

successfully then Theseus should display a white sail on his ship. This would signal 'mission accomplished'. Should Theseus die, and break his father's heart in the process, the returning survivors should hoist a black sail.

As is now well-known Theseus did indeed kill the Minotaur. This was only accomplished because Theseus was able to seduce Ariadne, the daughter of King Minos. Ariadne explained to Theseus that the Labyrinth in which the Minotaur dwelt had been designed by Daedalus, the master-craftsman. None who entered the infamous maze ever found their way out unaided – even if they did not have a brief and fatal meeting with the cannibalistic Minotaur.

However, the love-struck Ariadne made sure that Theseus had all the aid he needed. She provided him with a sword with which to kill the monster, and just as importantly, a skein of wool which Theseus could unspool behind him and so find his way out of the Labyrinth afterwards.

As her reward for organizing the killing of her monstrous step-brother all Ariadne asked was that Theseus take her as his companion when he left Crete once more. As we have seen earlier Theseus kept his promise and took Ariadne from Crete – only to abandon her on Naxos.

Doubtless Medea, who was at this time temporarily domiciled in Tyre in Phoenicia, heard of this treachery with the grim satisfaction of one who has predicted bad news and is proven right. She had read Theseus as trouble from the moment she saw him and would therefore have been completely unsurprised that he had used and then abandoned the trusting Ariadne.

On the other hand, Aegeus never got to discover that his son was a total rat. This was because on approaching Athens Theseus 'forgot' that he still had a black sail hoisted on this ship. Believing that his son had perished in the attempt to kill the Minotaur, the despairing Aegeus threw himself into the sea.

There were several consequences that followed from the perfidy of Theseus. The first was that the sea into which Aegeus cast himself has been called the Aegean Sea ever since. Secondly, once she found herself abandoned on Naxos, the despairing Ariadne contemplated hanging herself. (Some versions of the myth maintain that she did just that.) However, the more general opinion is that the god Dionysus persuaded Ariadne not to go through with it. This was because Dionysus was as smitten with love for Ariadne as she had previously been smitten with Theseus. Dionysus being an altogether more honourable character than Theseus, he and Ariadne eventually got married.

Thirdly, with his father dead, Theseus became King of Athens by popular acclaim – which may have been the point of hoisting a black sail in the first place. If Aegeus had not been driven to despair and suicide then Theseus would suffer nothing worse than a severe parental telling-off. If Aegeus did kill himself then Athens was there for the taking. It was, in modern parlance, a low-risk percentage play - and one that paid off handsomely.

Theseus went on to demonstrate his despicable character by raping and kidnapping several more women. One such kidnapping - of an Amazon – brought the wrath of that tribe of female warriors down upon the city. This did not cause Theseus to alter his

AFTERMATH

behaviour, indeed if anything, he became more extreme. When visiting Sparta, he lusted after the pre-pubescent Helen (later of Troy) when he saw her dancing with her friends. He promptly abducted her also.

When the outraged Spartan army started tearing Athens apart to find their lost princess, Theseus was nowhere to be found. He had gone to the Underworld to attempt an even more insane kidnapping – that of Persephone, the wife of Hades himself.

It was at this point that the career of Theseus as a sexual predator came to an end. He was petrified when Hades discovered his kidnap plot – literally because the King of the Dead began slowly and sadistically turning Theseus to stone. Freed by the good offices of Hercules, Theseus returned to Athens. There he found the population in no mood for explanations, bruised and furious as they were after their rough handling by the Spartans. Theseus died in exile.

We return from this slight digression to what had been happening to Medea in the meantime. The little we know comes from the Hyginus (*Fabulae* 26 &27) and the cryptic summary of Diodorus Siculus (*History* 4.55-56). While the two writers disagree on the exact details, enough material remains for a highly speculative reconstruction of events, which is given below.

The death of Aegeus did not help Medea, since Theseus was hardly likely to welcome his would-be murderer and her sons who had a legitimate claim to his throne. So, Athens remained out of the question as a refuge. The King of Corinth, Hippotes, hated Medea with a passion. Therefore, anywhere that could possibly extradite her into the power of the vengeful

Corinthian King was also out. Iolcus might have been a possibility since Thessalus, the oldest child of Medea and Jason, was now ruler there. On the other hand, the people of Iolcus had less than fond memories of Medea. Her arrival in that little kingdom would probably serve only to destabilize the rule of her son. For the moment Medea was stuck on the Eastern shores of the Mediterranean. It seems though that Medea used her time in exile to develop a web of contacts across the many states of Greece. She had influence and used it to obtain early notice of opportunities and dangers that might present themselves.

Greece might be closed off as a possible refuge, but what about her ancestral homeland of Colchis? True, Medea had originally left Colchis in a hurry (she had never left anywhere any other way), but Colchis was no longer the homeland she had fled. For a start, she had left a long time ago and a new generation might remember her with less bitterness – especially as the usurper Perses was not very popular. The people might welcome the return of Aeëtes and his family. One indication of this was that Perses, alleging that he was following the instructions of an oracle, had issued a decree ordaining death for any members of the family of Aeëtes who tried to set foot in his domain. This grim decree was to result in a comedy of errors deserving of an opera in its own right.

The story began when Medea's son Medus, now an impetuous teenager, decided to breach the travel ban imposed by Perses and see the situation in Colchis for himself. Since Medea was understandably protective of her surviving children, Medus waited until his mother was abroad and sneaked away. (Medea was courting several oriental kings with an eye to taking up residence in one of their domains.)

Sadly, Medus had underestimated how closely the paranoid Perses policed his borders. He was promptly captured. Working on the principle that a delayed execution was better than immediate death, the quick-thinking Medus claimed that he was actually Hippotes, King of Corinth, come to create a mutual-defence pact against the diabolical designs of Medea and her family. It was improbable that a king of as powerful a state as Corinth would just turn up unannounced. But it was definitely possible that the heralds announcing the coming of the king had not completed their journey. (As Jason and the Argonauts had demonstrated, getting to Colchis was no easy trip.)

Because Corinth was a powerful state, Perses could not take the risk that he was about to kill its king. Instead, he dispatched messengers to Corinth saying that he had someone in his custody who claimed to be Hippotes – could the Corinthians urgently confirm by return of messenger that this was indeed the case?

This was where Medea's web of informants and diplomatic contacts came in handy. Once she heard that Perses was holding Hippotes, she saw an opportunity to dispose of one enemy and discomfit two others. Medea had one huge advantage - thanks to her grandfather's chariot she could be in Colchis even before the messenger of Perses had reached Corinth. However, for some undisclosed reason she made one stop along the way.

This is revealed in an interesting aside mentioned here by Hyginus (*Fabula* 26) who says that while

MEDEA, QUEEN OF WITCHES

Medea was on her way to Colchis, she made a quick detour to visit the grave of her brother Absyrtus. The purpose of this visit is not given – it may have been to gloat, or possibly for a moment of nostalgic regret. On her arrival she discovered that the people in the town nearest the tomb were suffering from a plague of snakes. Rather in the manner of the Pied Piper, Medea gathered all these snakes and re-housed them within the tomb itself. 'They remain there to this day', Hyginus warns, 'and any who venture too close pays with their life.'

What we probably see here is a bronze-age tomb which became infested with snakes – quite possible because such locations are ideal for serpent colonies. Given that the location was on Medea's itinerary it is unsurprising that the phenomenon became linked with the town's most famous visitor. (One Arrian of Nicomedia reports passing by this tomb in AD 130, about a thousand years after Medea's brother was placed within.) Medea's expertise with snakes is noted elsewhere by an obscure writer of later antiquity called Servius Honoratus, who alleges that at some point Medea taught the art of snake charming to a tribe of Italians, who honoured her thereafter with the title Medea Anginita. ('Medea of the Serpents.')

Where Medus had simply blundered into Colchis, his mother was much more subtle. Once she had arrived and dismissed her dragon chariot, she made no attempt to hide the fact that she was in the country. But she did not arrive as Medea. Instead, she adopted the guise of that priestess of Artemis who had spent much of the previous decade in Athens inveighing against Medea and all her works.

AFTERMATH

In an audience with the King this 'priestess' assured Perses that his prisoner was not Hippotes but Medus, the son of the dreaded Medea. Let the King but produce the man and she could identify him immediately. After all, in Athens the priestess had seen Medus often enough.

Medea, of course, was expecting that Hippotes would be produced. She would then identify him as Medus and the annoying Corinthian King would be executed. As a bonus this would considerably sour relations between Perses and the Corinthians and the blame would fall squarely on the 'priestess of Artemis' who had made the false identification. For Medea this was a win-win-win situation. Another king would be added to her list of regicides, Perses would face extreme sanctions from the Corinthians and that irritating priestess of Artemis would, at the very least, have a lot of explaining to do.

It doubtless came as a shock to both mother and son when the prisoner was duly produced and turned out to be exactly whom the 'priestess' had claimed him to be - Medus, son of Medea. Not at all dismayed, Medea stuck to her original plan. She had come to make a false identification and she would follow through by doing exactly that. One can imagine Medus wilting under Medea's motherly glare as she carefully examined the prisoner. Her identity check complete, Medea turned to Perses and announced that his captive was certainly not Medus, but was indeed Hippotes, King of Corinth.

The endorsement of the supposed priestess was all that Perses required. He apologized profusely, and Medus the captive was promptly elevated to become

Hippotes the honoured guest. It may be that at this point Medea, in her role as an influential Athenian priestess, announced that she might be interested in negotiating Athenian entry into the fledging anti-Medean alliance which Medus had originally proposed while pretending to be Hippotes.

Thereafter Medea, her son and Perses closed themselves off in a quiet room for some very intense negotiations. So intense were the negotiations in fact, that only Medea and her son emerged from the room alive.

The people of Colchis were thus presented with an unexpected *coup d'etat*. Perses was gone. Medus was now in charge until his grandfather Aeëtes could take the throne again. If anyone wanted to disagree, the 'priestess' – now revealed as the terrifying Medea - would be happy to discuss the matter as soon as she had got the blood from her latest killing off her gown.

The nobility of Colchis had no wish to be added to Medea's scorecard, which currently stood at three kings dead by her hand, along with one prince (two if we count Jason), one princess and the allegedly invincible Talos. Add that no-one really liked Perses anyway and suddenly everyone was making enthusiastic plans for the return of Good King Aeëtes.

We do hear a bit more about the impetuous young Medus. It appears that he gathered an army and went on to conquer the homeland of his late uncle Perses.

Having secured the kingship there, Medus founded a settlement that later became the capital city of Ecbatana (Hyginus *Fabula* 275). According to Apollodorus, Medus eventually perished while attempting to expand

AFTERMATH

Medea at work as imagined by the eighteenth century Swiss painter Johann Füssli.

his kingdom into India. 'After conquering numerous barbarians, he called the land of his new conquests 'Media'. He met his end campaigning against the Indians.' (Apol. 1.9.28)

In the time of the Roman empire the writer Strabo agrees unequivocally 'Medus, Medea's son succeeded to the empire and left his own name to the country' (*Geographica* 11.13.10). This is in agreement with the view of Herodotus five hundred years previously, although Herodotus feels that the people of that country got their name directly from Medea 'Long ago these people were usually called Aryans but when Colchian Medea arrived from Athens they changed their name. That's how the Medes themselves tell it.' (*History* 7.62)

Another dubious etymology claims that Perses, Medea's other son by Aegeus of Athens, gave his name to the land of Persia. The Persians agree - at least to the extent that the modern peoples of that region reject the word 'Persian' as being of Greek origin and call themselves Iranians, a name rooted in their own culture. As far as we can speculate, Medea probably settled in 'Persia' with her son.

There's another reason for believing that Medea did indeed end up in southern Mesopotamia, and that's because she built a remarkable bridge in Babylon, according to Philostratus (*Life of Apollonius of Tyana* 1.25.) This would not have been her first attempt at such a structure, since a writer called Ampelius lists, in his wonders of the world 'The great double columned bridge called Hippoboton at Argos in Epirus which Medea ordered to be built.' *Liber Memorialis* 8. How and why Medea would have wanted to build a bridge in

AFTERMATH

Greece escapes the imagination, but it does show the lasting power of her name for later generations.

So, the story of Medea comes to an end, not with the thunderous climax of the Euripides play but with our protagonist quietly spending her final years in a land where her sons ruled adjoining kingdoms. It would appear that Medea never abandoned her pharmaceutical experiments. According to some writers – Hesiod and Cicero among their number – Medea leveraged her divine ancestry to become fully immortal.

In any case, living or dead, Medea made her way to Elysium, the equivalent of Paradise in Greek and Roman myth. Here in the so-called 'Isles of the Blessed' where the great heroes of myth mingled with nymphs and demigods, the restless Medea seems to have found happiness. She even took a young lover from the next generation of heroes. This lover was the son of the nymph Thetis and Pelias, Medea's old chum from the *Argo*. That son was, of course, Achilles who had been recently despatched from the land of the living in the Trojan wars thanks to an unfortunate poisoned arrow to the heel.

So (according to the Scholiast on *Ap. Rhod. Argon.* 4.815, the poet Ibycus, and also the lyric poet Simonides) we leave Medea and Achilles as they stroll together through the Meadow of Asphodel, in a match literally made in heaven.

Epilogue

Medea's Cultural Afterlife

Most of Medea's legacy can be blamed on Euripides. His depiction of Medea as a child-killer is gripping because, as in all the best tragedies, we are forced to recognize truths we would rather ignore. A mother is meant to be kind, self-sacrificing and nurturing – to the extent where society tends to forget that she is also a human being with her own issues and agenda. Medea veers wildly from the conventional script and so forces us to question its validity.

It would lessen our horror if we could imagine that the Medea of Euripides kills her children because she is deranged by grief. Yet Euripides takes pains to show that this is not the case. His Medea coldly works out the best way to hurt her treacherous husband and decides that this includes killing his children. So that's what she does. The fact that these victims are her children also and that the murders will hurt her terribly is considered by Medea to be acceptable collateral damage.

That's what makes the Medea of Euripides chilling. What makes her really terrifying is that the playwright explains - in lucid poetry - why mothers kill. Mothers, that is, who are not the murderous offspring of the Sun God but ordinary women of the kind who live down the street from you today.

Frederick Sandys, Medea 1868

Researchers such as Friedman in 2005. ("Child Murder by Mothers: A Critical Analysis of the Current State of Knowledge and a Research Agenda". *American Journal of Psychiatry*, 162) have converted the insights of Euripides into scientific research and others - particularly Dario Maestripieri - have shown that child murder happens among all primate mothers if the circumstances are right - i.e., very wrong. (*cf* "Assessment of danger to themselves and their infants by rhesus macaque (*Macaca mulatta*) mothers", *Journal of Comparative Psychology*, 109 1995.)

In other words, Medea might be doing the school run with her children tomorrow morning at your local kindergarten. She is still right here with us.

It is because this horror speaks so directly across the millennia that every generation has to come to grips with this aspect of Medea. We have seen the merciless Medea of Seneca's play from ancient Rome, but the same story was also told by Chaucer in the 14th century (in his *Legend of Good Women*). A modern *Medea* of note is the play of that name by Loher, a German playwright. He has Medea and Jason living as struggling immigrants in modern New York. Jason gets the chance to marry the daughter of a wealthy businessman, though this means abandoning Medea and her children ... .

Medea has also been the subject of over a dozen operas and plays from the Renaissance to modern times, such as Cherubini's eponymous opera, which (at the time of writing in 2023) is currently being staged by the Metropolitan Opera of New York. This opera was composed in 1797 and brought from relative obscurity by one of the 20th century's greatest sopranos, Maria Callas who sang the title role of Medea in 1953.

The frequent appearances of Medea on the stage testify to the enduring fascination with her character.

Visually Medea has remained in the public eye ever since she first appeared on Greek vases over 2500 years ago. Reubens, Turner and Rembrandt have all put scenes from Medea's life on canvas, as have dozens of other artists. In print today there are enough modern musings on Medea to fill a book or two, those books being Deborah Boedecker's *Medea: Essays on Medea in Myth, Literature, Philosophy, and Art*, published by Princeton University Press; and Hall, Macintosh and Taplin's, *Medea in Performance* 1500-2000, (University of Oxford).

Perhaps the most famous depiction of Medea is that by the Pre-Raphaelite painter Frederick Sandys (page 240). Inclusion of his 1868 oil painting appears to be almost compulsory in any modern text about Medea and unsurprisingly so. The painting depicts the fatal moment when Jason and his Argonauts arrive in Colchis. A stricken Medea clasps at her necklace as she works a spell at her censer. In the background a wounded dove drops from the sky while a bat is darkly silhouetted against the moon above the *Argo's* sail. The mood of the painting is ominous and we see Medea at the moment when her life is about to change forever.

So why the enduring interest in this particular mythical spell-caster? It is not as if classical myth lacks other fascinating female archetypes – Circe, Cassandra and Antigone come to mind – but there's something about Medea. Indeed - once the calumnies of Euripides are discounted - despite all her crimes, one ends up with a grudging respect for the lady.

Perhaps the Roman poet Horace put his finger on it when he describes Medea as 'wild and untamed' – which tells us that Medea lived in a society which believed that women needed taming. Yet despite this, Medea walks her own path, defying the gods and men who try to control her destiny. When pushed, she pushes back - hard. Murderess, renegade, deceiver;

MEDEA'S CULTURAL AFTERLIFE

Medea might admit to being all these things. But she is never a victim.

Sources

Ancient authors referenced in the text (commonly used titles are in translation)

Aeschylus *Prometheus Unbound* 36
Ampelius *Liber Memorialis* 237
Antiochus *Legends of Iolcus* 155,156
Apollodurus *Bibliotheca* 128,235
Apollonius Rhodius *Argonautica* 2,10,24,28,32,35,38,40,41, 43,46-48,53,57,58,60,62,63,67,71,105,117,133
Appian *Mithridatic Wars* 1,6
Aristophanes *Frogs* 210
Athenodoros *Commentaries* 156
Chaucer *Legend of the Good Women* 241
Didymus *Scholia in Euripidem* 205
Diodorus Siculus *Bibliotheca* 26,204,213-215,219,230
Euripides 133,136 *Electra* 122, *Hippolytus* 91 *Medea* vi,141, 156,157,159,161-164,169,170,172,175,178,179,184,185, 188,195,196,200-202,204-206,208,209-211,216,238,239, 241,243
Herodotus *History* 2,3,142,237
Hesiod 238, *Theogony* 9
Homer 143, *Iliad* viii,103,133,136-139, *Odyssey* 121,135
Horace 2,243 *Carmina* 1
Hyginus 233 *Fabulae* 67,117,230,232,275
Ibycus and Simonedes *The Argonauts* 238
Kreophylus of Samos, epic poet 205
Mousaios *The Isthmia* 209
Ovid vi,125,127,128,133,157 *Fabulae* 67, *Metamorphoses* xi,12,117,118, *Tristia* 73,74
Parmeniskos *Scholia in Euripidem* 206,207

SOURCES

Philostratus *Life of Apollonius of Tyana* 237
Photius *Myriobiblon* 156
Pindar *Pythian Odes* 7
Ptolemy *Geography* 91
Ptolemy Hephaestion *New History* 156
Pausanias *Guide to Greece* 146,207,208
Plato *Phaeto* 6, *Minos* 100
Pliny *Natural History* 7,149
Plutarch *Theseus* 218,221,224,226
Propertius *Elegies* 2
Scholiast on Appolonius Rhodius' *Argonautica* 238
Seneca *Medea* vi,167,170,172,176,179,180,181,195,196, 201,205,241
Servius Honoratus *Commentary on the Aeneid* 233
Strabo *Geographica* 4,91,237
Thucydides *Peloponnesian War* 94,209
Valerius Flaccus *Argonautica* 10,23
Xenophon *Anabasis* 3,4

Modern authors (details given in the text)

Cherubini Opera 241
Boedecker, D: Academic paper 243
Freidman, S. *et al.* : Academic paper 241
Hall, E., *et al.* : Book 243
Kolman, R. and Zurab Zarkua: Academic paper 63
Loher, D.: Play 241
Maestripieri , D: Academic paper 241

Illustrations

Medea the Sorceress: Painting vi
Helle falls from the Ram: Fresco 19
Jason of Iolcus: Statue 22

Hercules: Statue 31
Hera and Athena: Vase 40
Cupid: Fresco 43
Jason and Medea: Woodcut 51
Jason and the Serpent: Vase 60
Death of Absyrtus: Painting 64
Falcata Sword: Photo M. Matyszak 74
Circe: Neo-romantic style painting 78
The Argo: Painting 88
Bull of Marathon: Vase 95
Talos: Silver didrachm coin 97
Santorini/Thera: Public Domain photo 108
Poseidon: Statue 114
Medea revivifies the goat: Vase 126
Pelias and family: Fresco 129
Athenian women: Vase 138
Funeral Scene: Vase 144
Atalanta: Mosaic 152
Jason and Medea: Painting 160
Corinthian Woman: Painted Bowl 163
The Acrocorinth: Public Domain photo 168
Glauce/Cerusa: Sarcophagus bas-relief 172
Sicilian amphitheatre: Photo Avinash Shah 181
Jason, nurse and children: Sarcophagus bas-relief 184
Vision of Medea: Painting 188
Medea with knife: Statue effect 198
Molossian Hound: Statue 211
Medea's Chariot: Vase 213
Theseus: Fresco 223
Medea at Work: Painting 236
Medea: Sandys painting 240
Theatrical performance: 19th century photo effect 242
Maps Colchis 8, Aegean Sea 1300 BC 150

Index

A

Absyrtus 14,64-76,79,233
Acastus 24,143,145,151-154
Achilles 20,21,25,35,37,84, 136,137,238
Acrocorinth, the 168
Adriatic Sea 67,73
Aea/Aia 4-7,17,38
Aeaea/ Isle of Circe 76
Aeëtes 11-14,16-18,34,35, 38-42,44-47,53-55,57,58, 61-63, 65,66,68-70,72,73, 75,76, 79, 81,87,94,105, 117,168, 178, 219,220,231,235
Aegean Sea 109,141,229
Aegeus, king 173-177,204, 218-222,225-227, 229,230,237
Aegina 109,151,153
Aeneas 13,21
Aeolus 14,16
Aesculapius 21
Aeson 20-23,71,115-117,120-124,147
Aethelia/Elba 77
Africa 89,101,107
Albania 120
Alcimede see also Aeson 21
Alcinous, king 67
Alexandria 63
Alps, the 89
Amazons 33,229
Anatolia 1,29,33
Ancaeus 38
Antigone 243
Antiphemoessa (see also Sirens) 84
Aphrodite/Cypris 41,43,80,85, 160
Apollo 87,107,207,209
Apolydon 207
Apsaros, river 4
Ares 17,34,35,38,41,44,45,54
Argos 237
Argus nephew of Medea 18,34, 35,44,45,47
  shipwright 24,26
Ariadne 50,228,229
Aries see also Golden Fleece 17
Arrian of Nicomedia 233
Artemis 58
  priestess of 221,222,233, 234
  temple/isle of 69,70,72,186
Aryans (See also Persia) 237
Asia 16
Asphodel 238
Asterios (see also Minotaur) 96
Astydameia 152-154
Atalanta 25,145,151,152
Athamas, king 14,15
Athena 26,39-41,76,87
Athens 94,96,109,146,151, 164,173-176,191,193,195, 203,204,209,210,218-222, 224-227,229,230,233,234, 237
Atlantic Ocean 77
Atlas, titan 9,91
Atreus, house of 131
Attica (see also Athens) 14, 109,218,221

Ausonia 77
Axion 21

B
Babylon 237
Bithynia 33
Black Sea - see Euxine
Boeotia 14,15
Boreas, sons of 32,33,169
Briseus 137
Brittones 6
Butes 85

C
Cadmus 15,72
Caesar, Julius 113
Callas, Maria 242
Calliste (see also Thera)108
Calydonian Boar 25,151
Cassandra 243
Castor (see also Pollux, Gemini) 21,25,169
Cato the younger 89
Caucasus Mountains 4,8,10,35,37,38,53
Centaurs 149,153,154
Cephistus, river 225
Cercetae tribe 6
Cerossus 75
Chalciope sister of Medea 14
   wife of Augeus 219,220
Chiron 21
Christopher Columbus 6
Cicero 26,238
Cicons 136
Circe 11-13,76-82,85,94,105, 157,186,196,243
Colchicum autumnale 2,10
Colchine 49

Colchis 1,3-8,10-14,16-18,20, 27,29,33-38,44, 47,48,53, 57, 63,66,69,70,73,81,87,110,112, 115,116,124,130,134,141,145, 147,161,163,169,199,213,214, 220,221,227,231-233,235,243
Constanta 74
Corfu/Drepane 73,87
Corinth 14,124,146,147, 150, 151,156,158,161,164,167,173-177,180, 182-185,191,192, 194, 207, 208,212-214,217-219,221,227, 230,232,234
   Gulf of 205
Corinthus, king 146
Creon, king 158,167-171,176, 178,179,183,185,191-193,205-207,214,215,217,219,227
Crete 11,24,50,76,93, 94,97, 98,100,101,105-108, 147,155, 157,161,227,228
Cretheus, king 113,115
Creusa/Glauce 158
Creusus of Corinth 146
Cronus 80,87,139,201
Cupid 27,41,42,44,52,82
Cypris (see Aphrodite) 160
Cyrus, king 3,114
Cytaesis 5
Cyzicus 29,30

D
Daedalus 228
Danube, river 66
Dardanelles 29
Dardanus, king 29
Delos 107
Delphi, oracle of 107,173,174, 218,225,227

INDEX

Deucalion 24
Diomedes 92
Dionysia, the 210
Dionysus 15,21,24,123,229
Dioskourias 4
Dodona, oracle of 26,76,217
Draco 100
Drepane/Drepna 87
Dysceladus 75

E

Ecbatana 235
Echidna 201
Elba/Aethelia 77
Electra 29,76,122
Elysium 238
Enipus, river god/Enipeas, river 113
Epirus 237
Eretria 156
Etna, Mount 85,86
Euboea 109
Europa 98
Europe 5,16
Eurysthenes, king 23,24,194
Euxine/Black Sea 1,29,30,34, 63,65,66,75

F

Furies, the 80,81,82,186,196, 200,213

G

Gaia 35,38,91,201
Gardiki Fortress 87
Gemini (see also Castor, Pollux) 21,25
Georgia 4,10,62
Geryon 92

Gibraltar 6,77
Glauce/Cerusa 172
Glaucus 12,120
Golden Fleece 6,59,61,68, 69, 83,115,141,143
Graces, the 139
Grava cave 87
Greece 14,20,37,44,59,65, 66, 73,75,76,82,84,90,94,96,100, 108,109,110,120,131-135, 143,146-148,155-157,167, 169,174,176,191,194,204,208, 209,220,231,238
Gyenos, river 4

H

Hades 49,121,230
  hounds of (see also Keres) 103
  kingdom of 107,210
Halicarnassus 2
Harmonia, tomb of 72
Harpies 33,201
Hebe 121
Hecate 10-12,14,42,46,48,49, 53,58,59,102,110,118,121, 134,148,211
Helen of Troy 25,136,230
Helios 11,12,24,80,157,173, 177,178,193,204
Helladic tribes (see also Minyans) 65
Hellas 50,58,88,120,134,148, 169
Helle 14-17,19
Hellespont, the 17,29
Heniochi tribe 6
Hephaestion 156
Hephaestus 45,83,86,99, 101, 153

Hera 23,24,26,30,39,40-44,48, 49,58,63,72,75-77,82-87,91, 98,115,132,138,139,186,205-209,217
   Hera Akraia 209
   Heraion 205-207
Hercules 6,20-22,24, 25,28, 30-34,37,49,54,82,92,93,96, 112,131,194,213-215,218,224, 230
Hermes 13,14,21,24,154
Hesperides, the 92
Hippoboton bridge 237
Hippolyta, Amazon Queen 92
Hippolyte 152
Hippotes, king 192,219,230, 232,234,235
Histria 67
Holitorum Forum 203
Hylas 28,31,33

I
Ida, Mount 139
Idomeneus, king 155
Illyria 72
India 237
Indus, river 6
Ino 15,17
Iolcus 20,23,27,39,52,83,109-112,115,117,120,124,130,132, 134,135,140,141,145-147,149, 151,153-155,158,161,192,227, 231
Iophossa 14
Isles of the Blessed 238
Ismarus 136
Issa 75
Italy 12

J
Juniperus Sabina Cupressacae 60

K
Kent 6
Keres the 103-105
Knossos 94,97,98
Kolchoi tribe 4
Korisson, Lake 87

L
Lamia 201
Leda 25
Lemnos 27,28
Le Ghiale beach 77
Libya 89
Linus, brother of Orpheus 25
Lynceus 169
Lyrnessus 137

M
Macabees 190
Malea, Cape 167
Marathon, bull of 11,95,96,
   plain 96
   king 146
Mars (see also Ares) 17
Medea Anginita 233
Medes 237
Medus 220,227,231-235,237
Megara 218
Melite 75
Mesopotamia 237
Midas, king 97,112
Miletus 135
Minos, king 11,94,96,97,99, 100,105,228

INDEX

Minotaur 11,50,76,96,227-229
Minyans 65,66,68
Mithridates, king 1
Molossian hounds 211
Moschi tribe 6,7
Moses 113
Mycenae 131
Myriobiblon 156
Mysian 33

N

Naxos 50,228,229
Neleus 114
Nemea 20
Nephele 14-17
Nereus 32
Neriads 36,84-86
Nero, emperor 157
Niobe 198
Nymphea 75

O

Oceanus 91
Odysseus 13,76,85,121,135
Oedipus 82,114
Olympics 23
Olympus, Mount 9,58,120,123,183
    Olympian gods 8
Oreia, Mount 120
Orestes 122
Orpheus 25,85,92,169
Othrys, Mount 120

P

Pakistan 6
Paris, Trojan prince 136
Parnassus, Mount 181
Pasiphae 11,24,76,94-96,105,157
Pasithea 139
patria potestas 203
Patroclus 136
Peleus 25,35-37,84,145,151-155
Pelias, king 20,22-24,39,114-117,124-129,131,132,140,142,143,151,153,169,171,238
Pelion, Mount 26,120
Pelops 131
Perachora 205,208
Persephone 59,230
Perses,king 13,18,65,73,220,227,231,232,234,235,237
Persia 3,227,237
Phaistos 97
Pharsalus 113
Pheasant/phasianae aves 5
Phasis 4-6,17,38,62
Philostratus 237
Phoceans 73
Phoebe (the moon) 10
Phoenicia 228
Phrixus 14,15,17,18,26,34,35,41,42,44,45,47,59,69,73,81
Picidae/woodpeckers 12
Picus, king 12
Pied Piper 233
Pindus, mountain and range 120
Pityeia 75
Pollux (see also Castor, Gemini) 21,25,169
Pompeii 43,223
Pompey, Gnaeus 1,3,4,7,113
Poseidon 11,24,83,85,90,93,95,113-115,218

Procrustes 224,225
Prometheus 8-10,36,37,83,98

R
Rembrandt 242
Remus (see also Romulus) 113,114
Reubens 242
Rioni, river 5,62,63
Ris, river 4
Romania 66,74
Rome 1,133,203,241
Romulus 113,114

S
Samos 205
Santorini/Thera 108
Sargon, king 113
Saronic gulf 109,205,222
Scarlett o'Hara 161
Schibkah-el-Lovdjah (see also Lake Tritonis) 91
scholia 204-206
Sciron 224
Scylax 4
Scylla 12,13
Selene 157
Semele 15
Seneca vi,133,157
Sesostris, pharaoh 7
Sicily 12,85,181
Sidero 115
Sinis the Pine Bender 224
Sirens 85
Sirius/Dog star 50
Sisyphus 115,146,157
Socrates 6
Somnos 139
Sparta 66,136,230

Sunion,cape 227
Syrtis/Gulf of Sidra 89

T
Talos 94,97-106,147,235
Tantalus 131,201
Temnos 33
Termerus 224
Thales 135,141
Thanatos 103
Thebes 15,183,194,213-215, 218
Thera 109
Theseus 21,50,51,218,221-230
Thessalus, king 155,231
Thessalia/Thessaly 20,23,27, 83,113,120,155
Thetis 36,37,83,84,152-155, 238
Thrace 27
Tomis 74
Triton 93,107
Tritonis, Lake 91,93
Troezen 174
Trojan War 24,84,138,148,238
Troy 20,136,207,230
Trozen 218,222,224
Tyenoson 4
Tyre 228
Tyro of Iolcus 113,115

U
Ulysses (see also Odysseus) 13
Uranus 80,87,201
Ursa Minor alpha, beta 106
Uruatu 7

INDEX

V
Vetii 43

X
Xanthika ceremony 155
Xerobios river 4

Y
York 241

Z
Zeus 8,9,17,24-26,33-37,39, 44,58,75,76,80,83,84,91,98,138,139,146,152,157,217
Zeuxippe 85
Zygi tribe 6

Also in the Unauthorized Biography series

Hercules
The First Superhero

Philip Matyszak

Hercules the superman, the monster-slaying machine, the myth. Who was the man beneath the lionskin headdress, and does he really live up to his legend? This unique biography tells the story of the first superhero from his traumatic birth to his dramatic death.

Hercules was more than just his twelve famous labours. He was a father, a lover, a leader of armies and a fine strategist. He was also a cattle-thief, a murderer and a rapist. Using ancient sources from early Greece to the Late Roman Empire, this detailed biography fleshes out the character of one of the most complex and flawed heroes of Greek mythology.

MMP
Monashee Mountain Publishing

www.ingramcontent.com/pod-product-compliance
Lightning Source LLC
Chambersburg PA
CBHW070529090426
42735CB00013B/2924